PATRINELLA COOPER was born in a bender tent near Manchester towards the end of the Second World War. She spent her infancy living in a horse-drawn wagon, travelling between Manchester and Liverpool. When she was four years old, nuns descended on the travellers and persuaded them to send their children to school. Her family therefore settled near a school while she was educated.

But at the age of seventeen Patrinella eloped. She and her new husband ran away to Essex, where they travelled around, supporting themselves by picking fruit and vegetables, hawking and fortune-telling. A few years later, they went to Australia, where they spent the next ten years living in parts of Victoria and New South Wales, fruit picking, opal mining, gold fossicking, sheep droving and working on the fairs (or 'shows' as they are called there), fortune-telling and running booths.

Several years after returning home to England, she and her husband found themselves living in Cambridgeshire, Lincolnshire and North Norfolk, doing seasonal agricultural work as well as hawking and Tarot-reading. This remains her lifestyle to this day.

Patrinella has been interested in the magical subjects described in this book for as long as she can remember – even as a tiny child – and was fortunate enough to be born into a traditional family who could satisfy her curiosity with their wisdom. Her uncle was married to a European gypsy who also taught Patrinella some of her traditional magic and, when Patrinella lived in Australia, she and her husband mixed with Italian travellers from whom she also learned many things.

Ke mandi dordi rom Gavin,
men peer miripens drum ketani

GYPSY MAGIC

A Romany Book of Spells, Charms and Fortune-Telling

PATRINELLA COOPER

LONDON · SYDNEY · AUCKLAND · JOHANNESBURG

7 9 10 8 6

First published in 2001 by Rider,
an imprint of Ebury Press · Random House
20 Vauxhall Bridge Road · London SW1V 2SA

Penguin Random House is committed to a sustainable future for
our business, our readers and our planet. This book is made from
Forest Stewardship Council® certified paper.

Printed and bound in Great Britain by Clays Ltd, Elcograf S.p.A.

The Random House Group Limited Reg. No. 954009

Addresses for companies within The Random House Group Limited can be found at:
www.randomhouse.co.uk/offices.htm

Illustrations by Robert Loxton
Designed by Lovelock & Co.

A CIP catalogue record for this book
is available from the British Library

ISBN 978 0 712 61236 4

Note from the Publisher
Any information given in this book is not intended to be taken as a
replacement for medical advice. Any person with a condition requiring medical
attention should consult a qualified practitioner or therapist.

Contents

Acknowledgements

To my dear friend Susann Fumero, who had the
dream that encouraged me to carry on with this book.

Also many thanks to Lucy Thompson for taking the
time to type the manuscript for me, in spite of all
her other commitments.

Introduction

The Romany Tradition

You may be forgiven for thinking that the Romany people are fire worshippers. Fire draws them like a magnet. Even in these days of push-button entertainment, there is something special about sitting round a good old 'yog' fire, the smoke-blackened kettle singing away on the kettle iron, ready to make endless cups of strong tea always required on these occasions.

The talk around the fire is wide-ranging: the incidents of the day, deals struck, horses good and bad, people met with, the exploits of the clever lurcher dogs, each tale more unlikely than the last, all the success and failures of the travelling life, punctuated by snorts of laughter, or expressions of sympathy. But when the logs settle lower in a shower of sparks, and the fire reflects a gentle glow on more thoughtful faces, it is not unusual for the talk to turn to the old question: just where do Gypsies come from?

The travellers themselves have several ideas on the subject. The more educated subscribe to the current theory that we arrived from India in medieval times. Some propose that we came from the lost continent of Atlantis, bringing great knowledge of healing and magic that has gradually been lost through the centuries of persecution, till only remnants remain. Some say that we came from Egypt, hence the name Gypsy, the last of the priestly caste of the old Egyptian religion, forced out by the New Order. Others firmly believe that we are descended from American Indians, and it is true that if you compare old photographs of the two peoples it is hard to tell which is which. I can remember my own grandfather declaring that we came over the western sea to trade horses. But when it is all thrashed out, the general opinion among travellers is that all over the world, from the beginning of time, there have always been travellers. Someone will always say, 'We were the first people God made, we've always been here, and we always will be, in spite of what the Gorga do to us!'

I myself am of the latter opinion. It is likely that early man was nomadic, following the herds of migrating animals and the seasonal fruits. When the general population settled down to build villages and raise crops, there would still be groups of wanderers making a living in the old way, travelling from place to place: traders, pedlars in all kinds of goods, the smith with his mysterious knowledge of working metal, making tools and weaponry, entertainers bringing a little light relief into hard lives, bards, shamans, fortune-tellers, healers. These people would band together for company and safety. They would intermarry, and in time form distinctive tribes.

According to the Channel 4 archaeology magazine *Down To Earth*, a Continental archaeologist has found a DNA link between present-day European Gypsies and ancient tribes of blacksmiths and entertainers, who she believes lived outcast from mainstream society. I know the much publicised, historically documented band came from India in the Middle Ages, but I believe that it was only one of many tribes worldwide, and that these people must have intermarried with tribes that were already established in Britain before the Dark Ages.

Over the years, the travellers would become increasingly estranged from the settled population. Estrangement would bring distrust, distrust fear. The farmers would turn to new gods, suitable to the ways of people growing crops and raising animals, while the travellers would carry on the old traditions, remembering the old gods, practising magic forgotten by the settled population in their push for progress. The villagers would have needed the goods and services provided by the occasional visits of the travellers, but the travellers themselves must have been viewed with awe and suspicion.

The travellers for their part would grow to look with scorn at the settled people for their lack of knowledge, their fear of strange roads and deep forests. While the travellers lived in the open, sheltering only in tents, the villagers huddled in their groups of small huts becoming estranged from nature, growing afraid of the dark night. The travelling people developed their own laws, customs and taboos, many of which, based on strict laws of hygiene, are still adhered to by Gypsies today. These codes were based on observation, common sense and the need to avoid danger and disease on the road. In this way a gulf developed between the two peoples that has remained through the centuries. This is how I believe the Gypsy people were born.

Gypsy Magic

Whatever their racial origins, the Gypsies are justly famed for their psychic powers and the ability to curse or bring good luck to those that cross their path. Some say that these powers are innate, bred through a blood line of countless generations of psychics. This is certainly true, but it is also true that the very nature of the life led by a Gypsy puts him in a unique position to develop those powers naturally.

He observes the wonders of the night sky, and the miraculous workings of the earth. He sees the secret, sometimes uncanny behaviour of the animals and respects them for their brains and cunning. Each day brings a new revelation, which causes him to look at the world through shamanistic eyes.

To fully develop your own psychic powers, you must know that these powers are real. You must *know* that magic works. I have used the word 'know' instead of 'believe' deliberately. Belief implies that there could be an element of doubt. You must be as sure of these powers as you are that the sun will rise in the morning.

The Gypsy knows that signs and portents bring messages and warning, because he has heeded those signs to good effect. He knows that curses and blessings work because he has seen the results. He knows that fortune-telling works; he has seen the vision become reality. He has seen or felt the presence of elves, ghosts, ghouls and other mythical creatures. All these things are just part of everyday life.

I hope this book will help you to develop confidence in your own psychic powers, or at least to become more attuned to the world around you, as in doing so you will lead a more joyful and satisfying life.

Discovering Magic

What is Magic?

The word magic can be used to describe a wide variety of practices, from simple spells to attract loved ones, to full-blown curses, to fortune-telling, healing, exorcism, and much more besides. Of course some things thought of as magic in the past are called science today, as no doubt much that is dismissed as superstition today may prove to have a scientific basis in the future.

Basically, magic works by using psychic energy directed by will power and visualisation to achieve a purpose. Ceremonies, spells, trances, candles, herbs, colours and perfume are all used to heighten emotion, increase visualisation and strengthen will power. If the emotion is strong enough, none of the above may be necessary to bring about the desired result. A spell is a kind of elaborate prayer, and it is always the most heartfelt prayer that gets the most dramatic answer. Psychic energy is neither good nor evil, black or white. It is innate in each and every one of us. Just like electricity, it is the way in which it is used that brings good or ill.

According to some schools of thought, there are two main streams of magical practice: high or ceremonial magic, and low or folk magic. I suppose the Romany way of doing things counts among the folk magic tradition, although some of the more esoteric magical thoughts and practices show a higher, perhaps hermetic influence. High magic uses lots of expensive equipment, robes and archaic language; folk magic uses the natural things about us, and simple words or spells. Practitioners of ceremonial magic claim that they are working to transform themselves into a higher state of being, while folk magic tends to more earthly needs, but in practice both ways can be used to achieve the same end results and I can't see that one is any better than the other.

Ceremonial magic and alchemy are largely based on Arabic and Hebrew traditions, and use the language and symbols appropriate to those traditions. The rituals are often complicated, sometimes taking days, even weeks to complete. The equipment used – swords, daggers, chalices, thuribles, and so on – is often, as mentioned earlier, expensive, as a glance at any occult paraphernalia catalogue will show. It sometimes amuses me that a shaman in the rain forest can get equally good results using feathers, bones and a cup made from an old tin can.

Witch craft, or wicca, uses magic, but is essentially a religion worshipping the horned god of nature and the mother goddess. It often uses similar equipment to that used in ceremonial magic, but their rites are usually performed 'sky clad', in other words naked. Some say this is to build up trust among the group, others that the psychic energy is stronger when there is no clothing to impede the flow, but I don't think that an energy that can be effectively sent to the other side of the globe can be impeded by something so fragile as a dress or shirt.

The Gypsy tradition goes back to the darkest reaches of time. It uses simple spells and rituals to harness the power of nature and of the elemental spirits that are all around us. The Gypsy people are as independent in thought as they are in other areas of life, and they don't believe that a clergyman is really necessary to intercede between a person and the 'powers that be'. Although most Romanies would profess a belief in the official religion of the country in which they reside, and indeed many are now born-again Christians, there is still a deep respect for the old ways. And why not, when everyday experience proves the efficacy of those ways?

Everyone has the right and the ability to use the natural power of nature for themselves, though of course, as with everything else in life, some people are more talented than others. The more experienced a person is in the ways of this paranormal, the more confident and thus the more successful he will become. The older and hopefully wiser a person grows, the more powerful he will become. The power should never be abused on trivialities, such as trying to impress others with your knowledge and ability, as this shows a complete lack of wisdom.

It saddens me when I hear someone say, 'I am into Buddhism at the moment', or 'into' crystals, or transcendental meditation, or whatever else the latest fad is. It reduces great philosophies to the level of making model planes, stamp-collecting or some other banal hobby, to be taken up with enthusiasm one day and forgotten the next. A person with this shallow attitude will never truly learn anything. He will never reap the benefits to be gained from following any magical path or tradition, least of all the Gypsy way.

It is a way that springs from the heart, and the deepest, most primitive instincts of man. It respects nature and man's place in nature. It teaches us to take joy in the moment.

I will tell you how the Gypsy tradition helped me to develop my own power, which in turn enables me to help other people through magic and fortune-telling.

Recognising the Power of the Universe

In order to use the great power that permeates every atom of the universe and breathes life into the world around us, we must first learn to recognise it. Too often we take the workings of nature for granted and ignore, or are ignorant of the everyday miracles that enable life to continue on this small planet of ours.

Living and working as we do in the controlled atmosphere of houses, offices, factories or shops, travelling in the comfort of motor vehicles, we lose touch with the rhythm of the seasons and phases of the moon that are so important to us all for food and growth. Even people engaged in agriculture are in a constant battle against nature instead of working with her, especially since intensive livestock rearing and the growing of engineered vegetable crops are now the norm.

Because civilisation has moved so far from the natural world, a conscious effort must be made to regain the sense of wonder that comes from observing the vitality in plants and animals, to feel the undercurrents in the air as subtle changes occur throughout the year.

Science has worked hard to uncover the secrets of the universe. Through modern techniques, what once was mysterious has become open, even commonplace. As a result the world has become rather two-dimensional, lacking the hidden depths that the human psyche needs to grow and flourish. For too many people life has lost its purpose; it has no meaning. They work hard, overeat, worry too much about their diet. They may take a holiday once or twice a year, and bring

Chapter One

up children, but too often there is an empty space where their souls should be.

They try to fill the gap with frantic activity, sports, hobbies, buying ever more expensive consumer goods, but there is a lack of respect and consideration, first for the environment, and then for each other. This leads to an increasingly selfish, crime-ridden society, and an earth that is slowly dying.

Although scientists would like you to think that they know just about everything there is to know about the workings of nature, the so-called solutions proffered often leave many more questions unanswered. For instance, the theory that the universe started with a 'big bang' doesn't explain where the original matter that exploded into the stars and planets came from in the first place. The mechanics of how a seed grows into a tree, or an egg into a bird can be explained but not how or where the spark of life that provides awareness comes from.

Don't forget that even something as accepted as Darwin's theory of evolution is still just a theory and may be disproved by further research. Scientists are constantly reassessing and discarding old truths as new data becomes available. Once you start to question the recognised dogma of our times you will have taken the first step to regaining awareness of the life force that is sometimes called the power of magic.

Learn to think and question. Have the
confidence to formulate your own theories.

12

Learn to See the Natural World

We have all seen lines of tiny ants scurrying about their work, oblivious of the giant human towering above them. Most of us are like the ants intent on our own affairs, unaware of the larger world around us. Open your eyes, become curious, nosy even. Notice the little things, the intricate fronds of a feather blowing along the ground. The different shapes and shades of the leaves. The subtle colouring of even the smallest wild flower. See the make-up of the rocks and pebbles: many have veins and patterns of different colours, sparkling with tiny crystals. The gravel on your drive may contain fossil shells; an old gatepost may have a miniature mossy garden growing in its cavity.

If insects are creepy-crawly things that make you shudder, try to overcome your revulsion and look at them with new eyes. They are each incredibly beautiful in their own individual way. For instance, many beetles have iridescent wings of gold, copper, turquoise or red. The eyes of moths flying to a lighted window reflect light like tiny emeralds or rubies, and even the hated spider comes in many patterns and colours.

> Try to become familiar with the patterns of the stars, the rising and setting of the planets, and the way that the phases of the moon affect your life. The moon controls the tides, the liquid in your teacup, even the crust of the earth itself. The changes of the moon can affect your moods, your health, your luck.

Notice the habits of birds: they do some strange things if you take time to watch them for a while. Even the family pets can have a surprise or two in store when you really take notice of what they are doing.

Feel the changing seasons of the year with your whole being. Sense the stirring of new life beneath the soil in late winter, as the plant world starts to waken, stretching roots and tentatively pushing out the first pale shoot of new growth. Share the excitement of spring, when birds and animals lose much of their shyness in the joy of mating and take pride in their new offspring, engaging in frantic activity as they desperately work to fill the hungry mouths. Relax and be thankful in summer, the time of plenty. Enjoy the scent and taste of fresh fruit. Make your own jam and wine; it is simpler that you may think. Take an interest in herbalism, and learn how even common old grass can heal certain ailments. Feel the wistful air of autumn, when the leaves change colour and die, rotting into the soil to provide nourishment for next year's new life. Winter has its own beauty, when the frost makes a silver net of every spider's web, and paints pictures on our windows. It is said that each snowflake has a unique pattern – why don't you take a magnifying glass and see for yourself? The frost and snow break up the soil, and the winter rains wash the humus into the earth, making an ideal environment for spring growth.

Life is an exciting cycle. Nothing dies without being reborn in some way. There is nothing in nature that hasn't got a use, or doesn't play a part in the overall pattern of life. Observing the small details of the world is second nature to the Romany. As well as bringing many small joys, it is an invaluable practical asset to someone living off the land at the mercy of the elements.

'That is all very well if you live in the country,' I hear you say. 'But what about town dwellers?'

Well, even a city has grass and trees. Pigeons, sparrows and starlings dwell on the rooftops, and there are places where you can see the sky. Neglected buildings have ragwort, ferns and buddleia growing in the gutters; cracks in the masonry are colonised by many varieties of enterprising plants, bright celebrations of nature in a grey world.

Try to surround yourself with life. If you haven't got a garden, fill your home with pot plants, ferns and grasses for luxuriant green growth, and the scented flowers of spring bulbs in season. You can even grow a miniature wood by planting chestnuts in a wide bowl.

A pet brings extra love and interest into anyone's life, as long as its needs are recognised and it is well looked after. If you can't have a dog or cat, what about a pet bird or even a fish? But remember that once you decide to own any kind of pet, or even plant for that matter, they are your responsibility; they can't look after themselves, but are dependent upon you for their welfare and

---

If you never see the sky, buy a calendar that shows the phases of the moon, as well as the equinox and solstice dates. Celebrate these dates in some way, perhaps by having a special meal suitable to the season.

---

happiness. It is very bad karma indeed to neglect this responsibility.

Whatever you do, wherever you go, use your eyes and your imagination. Notice the little things; really think, ask yourself, 'Why do things look as they do? Act as they do? Why that shape? That colour?' Don't take anything for granted, don't believe everything the experts tell you. Come to your own conclusions, from your own observations.

I don't mean that you should become a birdwatcher in the accepted sense of the word, or an expert on any of the subjects mentioned. Far from it. These things should just be part of your life as you go about your daily business. You don't have to know the name of every bird, plant, star or animal in order to appreciate their beauty and behaviour. Make your own names for these things if you want to. After all, someone just like you first named them in the past.

It's an old saying, 'The more you look, the more you see.' This is very true; there are many small adventures happening around you every day, some amusing, some tragic, some downright eerie. The more you see, the more you will find to wonder at, and the more you will become aware of the vibrant force that can be channelled to empower your life.

The Zee Energy and How to Use It

It is an inspired truth, common among most pantheistic and so-called primitive religions of the world, that there is a great primeval intelligence, an energy that gives life and form to every particle of the universe. The archetype gods and goddesses are all part of this great intelligence, each having dominion over a different aspect of life. Each star and planet is a sentient being, capable of manifesting in human form if necessary, as is each individual feature of the landscape. Each tree, each plant, even the stones on the ground are all given life and awareness through their roles in this great intelligence, as of course is animal life, from the most minute creature, to man himself.

Because all creation is part of this great god energy, everything is worthy of respect, and because all matter is connected through this energy we can tune into and use it through prayer and magic.

However, once we begin to lose respect for the rest of creation and overestimate our own importance, we become like cancer cells destroying the host body, and so bring about our own destruction.

We can see this happening now as we destroy the world a little more each day. Since the collapse of paganism and the rise of monotheistic, male-dominated religions, which are often more about controlling people than spiritual progress, the earth is no longer seen as the great goddess, mother of all life, but is just a commodity to be exploited. The watercourses are no longer protected as sacred. The trees, the lungs of the world, are cut down ruthlessly, often needlessly. The rich and diverse forms of life, insect, animal and plant, once so abundant, are destroyed one by one. The greedy few rape the world of her resources at an ever increasing rate, wasting the precious gifts she gives us, even poisoning our food, water and air to make themselves rich beyond imagination, while the rest of the world population struggles to survive.

The Zee Energy

The life force, the first primeval god, has been rediscovered several times in recent years. It has been called by various names: prana, viril, telluric energy, earth energy, the ether, among many others. Just as the blood in our bodies permeates every corpuscle of flesh but is concentrated in the veins, so the god energy is concentrated in ley lines, or the dragon paths of feng shui. These currents of energy are known to most cultures of the world by various names. As this is a book on Romany magic, I will use the name given by the Romanies: 'mi douvals zee' – the heart, or life, of God. From now on I will call it the zee.

The First Step

The first step towards performing any magic, or fortune-telling, is to recognise and harness the zee. This needs much less effort than you might expect; in fact it takes complete relaxation.

On a village green in Norfolk, there is a bench carved with the words, 'Sometimes I sits and thinks, sometimes I just sits'. The Gypsy people spend much of their time doing hard physical work, but when given the chance they are very good at both the above-mentioned activities, or should I say inactivities. You may wonder what this has to do with magic, but it is surprising what great ideas, what insight and inspiration spring from the subconscious when you sit for ten minutes without the distraction of radio or TV.

Quietening the Mind

Find a place that has a comfortable feel for you, a spot that feels welcoming, preferably outdoors. It is good to lie on the grass, or lean against a tree or rock, but sit on something comfortable if that feels better. If it is more convenient to be indoors, try to fill your room with harmony and life. Have growing things about you. Burn pleasant incense or oil, maybe a candle or two if that pleases you. The main thing is to feel relaxed. Don't try to clear your mind of thoughts: to try to do so consciously often has the opposite effect of making one tense. Let your mind range where it will. If you feel like looking around, look around! Notice the flowers, the sound of the birds, the wind through the leaves, the distant noise of traffic and people.

Gradually your thoughts will quieten. As your mind becomes still, imagine your body becoming less solid, your skin – the barrier between you and the outside world – melting. Imagine the zee energy shimmering all around you, permeating the earth beneath, the air above you. Feel the zee tingling around your body like electricity.

Take slow, deep breaths, drawing the air down into your stomach. With each breath visualise the sparkling zee being drawn into your body through every pore, through the soles of the feet, palms of the hand and crown of the head.

Continue in this way until the zee fills your whole body with vibrant glowing energy, and you feel yourself bursting with light. Now gradually close the barriers between you and the world again, to enclose the zee energy within your body. Feel your skin become solid again. Gradually the light drains from the extremities towards the torso. Then concentrate the light into a glowing ball situated in the region of the solar plexus. Concentrate your mind for a few moments on the reassuring feel of this ball of light, your own power house of energy, then darken it with an imaginary cover that will keep it safe, deep inside yourself until it is needed.

Do this exercise whenever you can, ideally every day, though of course this may not always be practical. Don't worry if you can't complete it every time; I have even been known to fall asleep halfway through. Just sitting quietly for a while is of great benefit to the psyche, so the time is never wasted.

The Chakras

Once you feel confident in your ability to get the most out of this quietening exercise, it is time to take the next step, which means activating the chakras. Chakras are concentrated points of energy. There are many chakras all over the body, but we will focus on the seven major chakras that are placed at intervals in a line roughly corresponding to the spinal column.

Some cultures picture the chakra as a spinning wheel or sun, others as a flower, a lotus or rose, its petals unfolding as the chakra is activated. Each chakra has its own colour and function as laid out in the following table.

Crown of head	violet	Spiritual lessons, psychic power, complete understanding, fulfilment.
Brow	indigo	Telepathy, mediumship, psychic communication, intuition.
Throat	electric blue	Psychic change and control, creativity, healing.
Heart	green	Love, growth, wealth, generosity, nature.
Solar plexus	yellow	The most important chakra. Helps control and direct energy effectively.
Spleen	orange	Will power, intelligence, logic.
Root of spine	red	Vitality, sex drive, personal attraction, power.

Activating the Chakras

Complete the exercise for quietening the mind, but instead of 'darkening' the concentrated ball of energy, visualise it moving to the base of the spine, to the root chakra. Imagine the chakra coming alive with a glowing red light, opening like a flower or spinning round like a wheel, whichever feels right for you. Concentrate for a while on the feeling as the red energy gets stronger and stronger. Then take the ball of energy up along your spinal column to activate the chakra situated in the area of the spleen in the same way. This time, imagine the energy as warm orange.

Once again move the energy up the spine to the solar plexus. The energy here should be a lovely yellow. Pay particular attention to this chakra as it is the key to unlocking and directing the power of the other chakras.

Move the energy in the same way up to the heart area. This time the chakra should be a clear emerald green. Continue moving the energy up to the throat chakra, which is electric blue. Next the brow chakra should be energised. This is situated in the region of the so-called third eye, and is pictured as indigo blue. Finally the zee energy should be concentrated on the crown of the head. This chakra is a beautiful clear violet.

For a while visualise your body alive with a radiant rainbow of zee energy pouring from the opened chakras. The rainbow permeates the aura surrounding your body. Enjoy this feeling for a while then gradually close down each chakra in reverse order, from the crown to the solar plexus, then from the root up to the solar plexus. Finally visualise the solar plexus closing, leaving your original ball of energy, which you should 'darken' as you did in the exercise of quietening the mind (page 20).

When you do this exercise properly, you can physically feel the chakras throbbing or glowing inside the body. It may be difficult to get to this stage at first, but just concentrate on each chakra in turn for as long as you feel able to without strain or losing interest.

Even when you become proficient in this exercise there may be times when it is difficult if not impossible to activate one or more of the chakras. This could result from an emotional problem, some nagging subconscious worry, or just tiredness. Don't try to force things, and don't be discouraged. Do the exercise as best you can, when you can. It will always bring some benefit.

All psychic and magical activity uses zee energy that is transformed and directed through the chakras. Sometimes, usually under very emotional circumstances, this can happen unconsciously. For instance, the truly heartfelt prayer of someone in great need or danger can focus the energy with miraculous results, but for the most magical purposes the zee must be directed through the chakras consciously. The practice of the above exercises will make this easier until, with time, it will become second nature.

When one feels a strong emotional reaction to another person or situation, a sudden rush of love, joy, protection, sorrow, fear or intense dislike, the feeling is not just in the mind but is felt in other parts of the body such as the chest or the pit of the stomach. Learn to take note of these feelings, and you will find that they originate in one or more of the chakra areas.

The Gypsy knows that these raw emotions are powerful stuff when directed properly, especially love and hate. That is why a Gypsy curse or blessing is so effective.

Blessings, Charms and Other Ways to Attract Good Luck

When the average person wishes someone good luck, it is said in a light frame of mind and has little or no effect. But a Gypsy wish or blessing is given with intent, backed by occult ability to make it effective.

My great-grandmother Ella Cooper was a darling old lady, welcomed wherever she went. When asked how a sprig of heather or bundle of pegs could bring good luck, she would reply, 'It's not what you buy, my dear; it's the wish that comes with it that brings the luck.' She also believed that a sincere wish is a form of prayer. I am sure she was right on both counts.

Sometimes when I am out with my basket selling door to door I will be told, 'Well, I haven't had any luck since I bought from you last time.' But further conversation reveals such things as an exam passed against all odds, a breadwinner keeping their job when workmates were made redundant, a car crash from which the occupants miraculously escaped unscathed, a burglary interrupted before anything was taken. The list is endless. Sadly, what most people mean by not having any luck is that they have not won a fortune.

In this greed-ridden society, with its emphasis on designer labels and judging people by what they own, it is easy to forget that there are many kinds of luck. Many people in the world would consider themselves very fortunate to have a full belly and a warm bed, but I have met lots of people living in large comfortable houses, with nice clothes, the latest car, a loving partner and family and several holidays a year, who still moan that they never have any luck.

Of course it would be nice to come into a fortune. While money doesn't buy happiness, it can certainly relieve some very pressing worries, and, as the old saying goes, you can at least be miserable in comfort. However it would do us all good to count our blessings from time to time. Having said that, though, we all want to attract a little more luck into our lives, and buying something from a Gypsy is a good start.

Lucky Charms

As well as pegs, potpourri and other little things, I sell a selection of lucky charms. These are especially made for the Romany people and all have a special meaning. I find that people are usually subconsciously attracted to the one that represents certain qualities needed in their life at the time, for instance a dog for friendship, a boot for progress, or a wishbone for a dream come true. The charms are given life, or charged, by being blessed 'to put the luck in them'.

It is no use buying a charm only to put it away and forget it. It should be kept close to the owner in a purse or pocket, or worn around the neck, and it should be handled often, always with a feeling of happiness and hope. The greater the certainty that the charm will bring good luck, the more effective it will be. The opposite is also true. If someone buys a charm thinking, *How can this bring me luck? I am never lucky*, and always looks upon it in a negative way, of course it won't work – how can it? The charge will soon fade and die.

Lucky Omens

There are lots of everyday items and little ceremonies that can attract good fortune into your life:

Finding a four-leaf clover is a good sign of course, especially if you are just starting a new venture. The leaves each have a meaning: health, wealth, love and fame.

In autumn, when the leaves are falling, try to catch an oak leaf before it touches the ground. Keeping it in your purse or wallet ensures it will never be empty.

Never walk over a lost coin in the street. Pick it up and spit on it saying, 'See a penny [or whatever it happens to be], pick it up, all day long I'll have good luck.'

Always wish on the first star to appear in the sky, as well as on a shooting star. You should also wish on a rainbow. If you are lucky enough to be where the rainbow touches the earth, you will be especially blessed for six months.

Respectfully greet a white horse, a hare, a fox, magpies, rooks

---

The places where water comes from the earth, such as wells and springs, have always been held in reverence. Make a small offering when you come across such a place: a coin or even a pin or hairgrip thrown into the water, or a scrap of cloth tied nearby. The Romanies like to leave red wool for preference. Say a little prayer of thanks for the life-giving water and also ask the spirit of the place to bless you with good fortune.

---

and crows. These creatures are touched with magic.

Always have respect for nature in all her forms. The plants, trees, rivers and rocks – these things are full of their own wisdom and have seen countless generations of man come and go.

Try to keep an eye open for the first appearance of the new moon in the sky. The lovely silver crescent of the new moon always fills me with awe and brings optimism for the coming month. Bow reverently three times, then turn your money over three times. Praise the beauty of the moon, and ask for her blessing in the month ahead. Likewise the full moon brings good fortune to those who ask her for her blessing.

All this may seem like senseless superstition, but these practices are remnants of ancient beliefs, and they really do work. They will also help you to get in touch with the zee energy, and to look at the world in a more magical Gypsy way.

Lucky Stones

Stones are part of the great consciousness and have their own kind of awareness. When you are walking along a stone or pebble may catch your eye for no apparent reason. Always pick it up. It may want to be moved. Keep it for the day for luck. You can spit on it and say, 'Little stone I pick you up, all this day you'll bring me luck.' At the end of the day leave it wherever seems appropriate.

Sometimes a stone may seem unusually magical. It may be patterned in a way that has a meaning for you, or it may just feel particularly good. Keep this stone as your amulet for as long as you can. One day you will lose it, but don't worry – another will soon take its place. A stone shaped like an animal or an object or maybe with a picture of some creature upon it was once considered to bring power over whatever was depicted. I have met an old Romany horse dealer who always carries a flint with a pony clearly pictured in the marks on its surface. He swears he wouldn't part with his stone for any money, believing it has brought luck in dealing and business and also possesses the power to calm a nervous horse.

Of course stones pierced with a natural hole have always been prized. Keep tiny ones in your purse, and thread pebble-sized stones on a string to hang by the fireplace, in the kitchen or by the entrance door. If you are fortunate enough to find a really large stone with a hole, place it outside, next to your door or gate.

But a word of warning: never remove a large stone that is well embedded in the earth, or is next to a natural feature such as a spring or old tree, or near a well. If a stone seems to enhance the scene in which it is set, it is probably important to the energy of the place and should be left where it is.

Many people have a favourite object or ornament that makes them feel good whenever they see it. This kind of thing can be used as a good luck battery for the home. The object can be charged in the same way that a duk koor can be charged for protection (see Chapter 5, page 53). This time imbue the object with good luck and optimism. Whenever something nice happens or you are feeling happy stroke the object and tell it all about it. Any object that appeals to you can be used in this way; I have seen a Buddha, a little grinning frog, a statue of Lakshmi, the Indian goddess of good luck, a lucky black cat made from plaster brought back from a holiday in Blackpool, a small log of wood with a smiling face embossed in the knots and ridges of its bark. A friend of mine even has a shiny black teapot that once belonged to her grandmother that has been charged for this purpose. You can also do the same thing for the workplace to attract success.

Good Luck Talismans

Nowadays both speech and the written word are taken very much for granted, but this was not always so. Creation myths from many different cultures tell how God brought the world into being with a word, and knowing the correct name of a person or thing was to have power over it. Writing was a sacred tool as well as a means of communication. The symbols attributed to the gods and other powerful beings have a lot to tell us about the essence of those beings.

Talismans make use of writing, names and symbolism to make a kind of powerful circuit board for attracting good fortune or repelling evil, and they have been used for centuries. They can be etched on the appropriate metal or stone, or can be written on clean paper or parchment. Ideally, this should be done on the correct day and time for the intended purpose.

Probably the most familiar talismans come from the Cabalistic tradition, but every culture has its own versions that are equally powerful. These include runic, Hindu and Celtic versions, as well as the inventive pictograms of chaos magic. Our Romany tradition has its own powerful symbolic talismans but also makes full use of those from other cultures. You can quite legitimately create your own talismans using names and symbols that strike a cord in your own psyche.

Making Your Own Talisman

To make your own talisman, decide which word or image is the best one for your chosen purpose. Carefully copy out the design on clean paper or parchment, using pens not used for any other purpose. As you work keep in mind the effect you want the talisman to bring about.

Using colours and perfumes appropriate to the talisman (see Chapter 6) and at the correct hour, cover a small table with a clean piece of cloth. Place three lighted candles in a triangle. Put lighted incense on the left side, and a small bowl of water into which a few drops of perfumed oil and a little salt have been sprinkled on the right. Place the talisman in the centre of the triangle.

Imagine that you are in the middle of a circle of golden light. The candles make a triangular pyramid of even more intense light pouring down upon the talisman. Pick up the talisman and pass it three times over the flame of the middle candle, then three times through the incense smoke. Finally sprinkle it three times with the water. As you do this, say slowly and with purpose, 'I call upon the powers of the universe, the guardians of the four directions and the elements of the earth to witness my work and bring power to my purpose.'

Put the talisman back in its place on the table. Visualise an intense ray of light beaming into the talisman. Call upon the ruler of the talisman by name and say, 'Fill this talisman with your great power. May it be invincible and unstoppable in its purpose. May it bring me [or the name of the person it is intended for] good luck, success and protection.' At this point you can include a few words stating exactly what you want from the talisman. As you speak, imagine the writing on the talisman being charged with power. It is filled with a sparkling electricity. When you feel that the talisman is fully charged say, 'I thank you for your blessing and your help. May we part in peace and meet again in joy and love.'

Put the talisman in a little bag made of some material of the correct colour. It should be worn close to the person or kept with you in a purse or pocket.

At the end of this chapter I have given some examples of talismans for more common purposes as well as tables of perfumes and colours, but if you want to learn more there are several good books devoted to the subject (see Further Reading).

Blessing Holders: the Gypsy Parik-til for Luck

The Native American people still make medicine bags, which are worn on thongs around the neck. This type of amulet has been known in many cultures since the dawn of time and is much used in Romany magic. We call it a parik-til, a blessing holder.

Making a Blessing Holder

To create a parik-til, a small drawstring pouch is made in the appropriate colour for the intended purpose. Into this goes various little objects: herbs, stones, feathers, sometimes a charm or piece of paper inscribed with a simple spell. This list is endless; it is only important that the objects seem sympathetic to your purpose. These things can be scented with a few drops of perfumed oil.

The whole should be dedicated in a similar way as given for the talisman. Follow the steps given for the talisman dedication, but place the contents of the parik-til in the centre position on the table, together with the bag. Put the objects in the bag before passing it through the incense smoke and over the candle flame and sprinkling it with water, as you did with the talisman. Then carry on in exactly the same way as previously explained.

Here are a few examples of parik-tils for different purposes, but there are no hard and fast rules. You are only restricted by your own imagination and what your own instinct tells you.

A Parik-til for Health

Gather a sprig each of St John's wort, woundwort and self-heal, along with a twig or leaf from an oak tree, a tiny water-worn pebble, which should be round or disc-shaped and preferably have a reddish or orange hue, a light downy feather and a scrap of red flannel or woollen cloth. Bind the herbs and feather round with a cord made from plaiting red, orange and light blue thread together. Wrap the herbs together with the pebble in the red cloth and tie with another length of the plaited cord. Put in a red drawstring bag, and perfume with a few drops of sandalwood or myrrh oil.

A Parik-til for Love

Collect a few rose leaves and petals, three or seven apple or pomegranate seeds and a small gemstone, which can be turquoise, emerald or aquamarine (this doesn't have to be genuine; if you really can't obtain one, use coloured glass). Also gather a heart-shaped object (maybe a charm or a naturally shaped stone), and a feather from a dove or pigeon or gathered from any used bird's nest (but only if the nest has been abandoned because the chicks have flown). If there is someone you particularly want to attract, include some dirt over which they have walked; alternatively, a scrap of clothing or something like a tissue that they have used will work. This only needs to be a thread or the tiniest thing. Tie the leaves and feather together with a cord plaited from red, orange and pink thread. Put together with the other objects into a pink drawstring bag. Perfume with rose or musk oil.

A Parik-til for Luck and Success

Collect leaves and twigs of the oak tree, including a small acorn if available, the petals and/or seeds of the sunflower, a piece of cinnamon stick, three cloves, a stone that feels lucky for you, a horseshoe charm and a little gold (for instance a broken bit of jewellery or an odd earring). Tie the oak leaves and twigs with a cord made from green, yellow and orange thread. Put with the rest of the objects into a green drawstring bag. Perfume with myrrh, benzoin or patchouli.

As you see, there are lots of ways to attract good luck, but more than that the rites and practices described will enrich your life in many subtle and unexpected ways. Why don't you try them for a while and see for yourself?

CHAPTER FOUR

The Power
of Wishing
and Spells

Guidance From the Gods

It may seem strange in a book such as this to talk about saying your prayers, especially in a chapter devoted to wishing and spells, but a wish is a kind of prayer, and a spell is just a more elaborate form of the same thing. When you pray, life can seem less of a worry, obstacles are cleared away, you gain more confidence and feel more joy in life.

By praying I don't mean the meaningless mouthing of prayers learned by rote in childhood, without a thought for what is actually being said. Prayers should be felt from the heart and directed properly. Not that there isn't a place for those childhood prayers if they have meaning for you, but putting your feelings into your own words may be more apt and sincere.

You should say a prayer of thanks for a new day, for protection when going on a journey, for help when facing a difficult task. A thank you for the food on your table doesn't go amiss, and will help you to appreciate how lucky you are. If you are worried or afraid, a prayer for help or protection can calm your fears. Say 'thank you' when you feel lucky or happy, have a grumble when disgruntled, and don't feel guilty about praying for money or other material things. There's nothing wrong with trying to better yourself, as long as avarice doesn't take over your life. You can pray for anything in any situation, but don't forget to be appreciative too.

Earlier I talked about the archetypal beings, the gods and goddesses. Each has dominion over an aspect of life. Christianity and other religions have patron saints, angels or other beings that serve the same purpose. For instance, Anubis in the Egyptian pantheon and St Christopher of Christianity both protect the traveller. Wayland Smith is a Norse god who will help when any type of machinery, metalworking and craftsmanship are involved. Odin, the Norse god of knowledge and communication, is roughly equivalent to Thoth (Egyptian), Hermes (Greek) and Mercury (Roman). Isis is one name for the mother goddess, the all-providing earth, but every culture has their own name for her. Even the Christian Church has had to bring this feminine principle into their hagiology under the guise of the Virgin Mary.

When you pray, you must first decide whom you are going to pray to; who would be the right being to approach with your particular needs? Picture this being in a setting that is natural to them, surrounded by the symbols, colours, perfumes and sounds you would expect to be there. Call them by their name three times, and add any other titles that you know them by. Invent your own name and titles for them if you wish to do so. Make your prayer sincerely, in your own words and with trust that it will be answered. Think about what you are saying. End by saying 'thank you'.

All this may seem quite complicated at first, but when you have had a little practice it only takes a few seconds. There is no need to pray out loud, though you can do so if you feel the need. It is entirely up to you.

Once you have made a habit of *really* praying, you will quickly find yourself becoming, like the Romany people, quite fatalistic.

When you ask the gods, or saints, as the case may be, for help, you can confidently leave things in their hands. I don't mean that you should sit back and do nothing; on the contrary. You should do your best to help yourself, but if you find your way blocked you can be sure that it is because what you are aiming for is not right for you. Something better is in the offing. After the initial annoyance you will find yourself able to forget disappointment and look forward to something better coming along. Everything happens for a purpose and your prayers will not always be answered in the way you expect.

Linda had set her heart on buying a particular small bungalow. Situated in open countryside with no neighbours except for the birds, it seemed ideal. She couldn't understand why, in spite of all her prayers, one thing after another arose to stop her exchanging contracts and making it her own. In the end she was forced to give in and settle for a house that she considered to be second best. Two years later she had occasion to pass the bungalow she had once hoped to make her lifelong home. It was now

The Gypsy people never worry if they take a wrong turn on the road, and will seldom turn back; you never know what adventures may be waiting along a strange road. If your car doesn't start in the morning, maybe leaving at your usual time would have involved you in an accident. If you miss the first bus, maybe you will meet a new friend on the next one.

overshadowed by a gas-fired power station that was under construction across the road.

Mandy failed an interview for a job that she had fervently prayed to get. A week later she landed an equally good post with better long-term prospects, and furthermore she met her future husband Alan working for the same firm.

Prayers are usually answered in a very positive way. Praying can protect you from harm and smooth your path in a remarkable way. I have known miracles happen through prayer, and many small worries eased. Once you realise the power of prayer it is like a weight lifting from your shoulders: things happen; you will be in the right place at the right time; you will find the person you need when you need them. Coincidence works to your advantage. If things do go wrong, help will be on hand. The gods are generous and want to help – what's more, they actually need your prayers – but always remember to thank them for their aid. They appreciate gratitude just as much as you or I.

Wishes

There's hardly a day goes by when most of us don't wish for something or other. Usually these are vague longings or impossible dreams put into words without hope of an answer. And it's a good job too, sometimes; after all, would you really like to sprout a second pair of hands, or have the floor open up and swallow you when you are embarrassed? The idea that wishes can come true is the stuff of fairy tales, but believe me wishes do come true.

Unlike a prayer, a wish is not directed to a particular entity: it is sent out into the network of zee energy rather like an SOS message transmitted over the radio to be answered by those best able to help.

To make an effective wish, find that quiet spot deep inside yourself as before, then concentrate on nothing except what it is that you want. Make your wish, putting all your heart and soul into it. Don't think about why you want this thing, or what you will use it for, just that you want it desperately. When you have made your wish, put it to the back of your mind in the knowledge that you have done your bit. The zee will take care of the rest.

There are places and objects that can help to make your wish stronger by acting as a kind of booster aerial. Try holding a lucky charm or a four-leaf clover, or wishing on a star, a rainbow or the moon when it is new or full. Some ancient stones and places are said to have the ability to grant wishes. Another person who wishes good for you with real intensity will be a wonderful booster, which is one of the reasons why a Gypsy can bring you good luck. A Gypsy knows how to use her psychic power in this way.

In fairy tales the hero or heroine usually only gets three wishes. Maybe this is because it is too easy to fall into the trap of wishing for trivialities, in which case the power will quickly wane and you will get nothing. Save your wishes for when you really need them. Above all, don't be too greedy.

> If you truly need or want a thing, if you wish hard
> enough it will come to you.

Protection Against Curses and Bad Luck

Unfortunately, of all the emotions hate is the one that is most likely to bring about immediate, effective results, especially when directed in the form of a curse. Even people who have no knowledge of or belief in magic, when goaded into wishing ill on someone who has annoyed them, are sometimes dismayed to find that their curse has worked. Hate, when targeted by a person who knows what they are doing, can be devastating.

The Gypsy Curse

Most people, on seeing a Gypsy woman selling lucky heather in town, will try to give her a wide berth, and are horrified if one should come knocking on their own front door. 'Well, you can't get rid of them once they catch you,' is the usual excuse, but it is often the fear of the Gypsy's curse that is the real reason.

I am sometimes asked, 'Why would a Gypsy want to curse someone she has never met before? And what makes them so persistent?' Well, put yourself in her place for a moment. From the day they are born, most Gypsy people meet with harassment and suspicion wherever they go. The fact that the Romany are a recognised ethnic minority, covered by the Race Relations Act, is largely ignored by the authorities, who are all too often prejudiced against the Gypsy people. Given this background, is it any wonder that a woman, or man for that matter, out hawking, trying to make an honest if unconventional living, when faced with nothing but hostility will sometimes snap and retaliate with a curse? The real wonder is that the Romany are usually very good-natured people. But make no mistake, these curses born of desperation and frustration do work!

Personally I would not curse anyone under those circumstances, though I can understand why others do. If I am hawking door to door, and people don't want to buy from me, that is their prerogative. If someone is so unpleasant that they make me want to curse them, then they are already cursed with a nasty disposition and a joyless life. There is no need for me to damage my karma by cursing them, too. Furthermore, I believe that you get back what you give out. In the circle of life it all returns with interest, so I would rather be pleasant and hopefully brighten someone's day.

Yet sometimes a curse may seem to be the only form of defence or retaliation open to those who are unjustly treated or persecuted by society. An extreme form of this is a 'gallows curse', which is called down upon their tormenters by the victims of murder or execution. The results of such a curse uttered in the last few agonised moments of life are often sudden and dramatic.

Perhaps the most famous example is the case of Jacques De Molay, last grand master of the Knights Templars, who was burned at the stake in 1314. Jealous and covetous of the Templars' power and riches, King Philip of France plotted with the Pope to bring the downfall of the order so that they could get their hands on the fabled Templar treasure, accusing the Templars of many heinous and unnatural crimes. The order was abandoned and many Templars killed, its leaders tortured and executed. Jacques De Molay cursed the Pope and the King from the stake, saying that they would both join him within the year. Forty days later Philip lay dead. The Pope died within twelve months.

In 1819 an ancestor of my husband's family, a young man called Billy Boy Craige, had a magnificent stallion. He had raised it from a foal; in fact, it could be said that boy and horse had grown up together. They were inseparable. When the lord of a great estate in Northumberland tried to buy the stallion, Billy Boy wouldn't sell. Angry at being thwarted, the lord accused Billy Boy of stealing the stallion and had him condemned to death. From the gallows Billy Boy cursed the lord, crying, 'Before my body is cold, you will be in hell!'

Of course the lord laughed, but, as he was triumphantly riding the stallion away from the gallows where Billy Boy was choking out his last few pitiful moments on earth, the previously well-behaved mount went wild and bolted into the woods, dashing his rider against the trees and killing him.

Several men, including the heir to the estate, were hurt trying to recapture the horse to no avail. However the next evening the stallion trotted docilely into the clearing where the Craige family were camped. They, of course, promptly packed and left that part of the country, taking the horse with them. To this day some members of the family still proudly own horses who are reputedly descendants of Billy Boy's stallion.

Ritual Curses

As well as curses made powerful by the emotions of the moment, there are ritual curses. A ritual curse is called down with deliberation and ceremony, and sometimes involves the combined power of several people. It is usually made to affect a place, event or whole generations of a family. Its power is very great and can last for centuries.

On 6 October 1997 it was reported in the *Daily Mirror* that Middlesbrough Football Club had called upon the services of psychic cutlery bender Uri Geller to raise a Gypsy curse. The club ground had been built on a traditional Gypsy stopping place, and the evicted Romanies had retaliated in the only way they could, with a ritual curse. The club suffered continuous bad luck from then on. I don't know if Mr Geller was successful in his endeavour, but it usually takes the know-how of a Gypsy to raise a Gypsy curse, and under the circumstances it is very unlikely that one ever would.

It is said that the famous steam rally at Blandford in Dorset was similarly cursed when a Gypsy family was refused entry into the event. They cursed the rally with seven years' bad weather, and indeed for seven years torrential rain turned the venue into a quagmire. It wasn't until the stated seven years were over that the event was held under clear skies.

The small town of Fakenham in Norfolk is well worth a visit on market day. The many stalls are varied and interesting, with a large section dealing in second-hand goods and antiques. Unfortunately, this event also usually suffers from bad weather. Legend has it that this is because of a curse put upon it by the people of Walsingham, the famous shrine village situated six miles away. It seems that Walsingham had a thriving market, bringing much welcome business to the town until Fakenham set up a rival market with the result that Walsingham suffered and the market died. So the people of Walsingham cursed the Fakenham market. To this day, no matter what the weather is like during the rest of the week, it almost always rains in Fakenham on a market day.

A ritual curse is a powerful and devastating thing. It takes knowledge and skill to successfully activate a ritual curse without danger of it rebounding back on to the sender, but it is easy, probably too easy, to curse someone in the heat of the moment. All the negative emotions – the hurt, hate, frustration and fear – are not just felt within your body but are tingling like electricity in the air around you.

These emotions are drawn into the body, just as the zee energy was in the exercise to quieten the mind (page 20), then concentrated in the chest area while the curse is formulated. The energy is then shot out like a bolt of lightning aimed at the target

---

Because it is so easy to activate an effective curse, many people on discovering their power do so and, lacking in basic wisdom, tend to show off by cursing all and sundry at the least provocation. Beware of falling into this trap.

An unjust curse can, and will, rebound most horribly upon the sender. Besides which, all this hate shows on the face, leading to what in days gone by was called 'an evil countenance', and it can even cause illness.

---

while the curse is pronounced. There is no need to utter the curse aloud, though this is often done; it is the thought turned into energy that does the work.

In normal life, the chances of actually being cursed are thankfully few and far between, but there are many situations where one may come up against potentially harmful energy. One often comes up against bad feeling, jealousy and ill will, which if strong enough can be harmful. Sometimes too, one may be in the presence of an emotional vampire. These people are usually very pleasant, normal, everyday folk. But a few minutes in their company leaves one feeling tired and drained. Somehow they seem to suck all the energy from the people around them.

Protection Against Curses

Luckily you can easily protect yourself from energy-draining people by forming a 'duk rak', a psychic shield.

Creating a Duk Rak

First, visualise the essential you, your soul, being hidden deep inside yourself, quiet and safe.

Mentally, put on an all-enveloping cloak, which covers you from head to toe. Nothing can penetrate it.

Finally, imagine that you are holding a shield. The face of the shield is brilliantly reflective. Rays of light dart from the surface. It reflects any harm back to the person who is sending it, making them a victim of their own animosity.

If you have practised the exercises given in the previous

chapters, all this will only take a moment. The stronger the visualisation, the more effective the protection.

Major buildings were once protected from ill luck by the burial of a human sacrifice in the foundations, and up to medieval times animals, often cats, were buried in the foundations or under the threshold stones of houses. Until quite recently children's shoes or bottles containing bent pins often served the same purpose. If you are lucky enough to own an old house and find any of these, or similar objects, be sure to put them back where you found them.

In late 1980s renovations were carried out at the Bull Hotel in a village near Dereham, Norfolk. The place was flourishing, and the landlord was well liked and prosperous. During the building work a child's shoe, dating from medieval times, was found bricked into a wall, and was donated to the museum at Little Dunham. And from then on things started to go downhill. The landlord's marriage broke up, his business suffered so much he had to give up the pub, and after a series of misfortunes the poor man committed suicide. The Bull has had several landlords since, none of whom have stayed long or managed to bring back the happy prosperity of only a few years ago.

Perhaps it is coincidence that the decline started when the shoe, the building's luck and protection, was removed. Who knows? I have heard recently that the shoe has now been returned to the Bull. It would be interesting to see if the luck returns as well, or has its unceremonious removal broken the charm forever?

Using a Duk Rak for Protection

There are several ways in which you can protect your home or property. For long-term protection, prepare several occult seals, 'duk rak' in Romany. These can be small wooden staves a few inches high, or stones with a flat surface. There should be one for each corner of your boundary, and one for each gate and door. These should be painted with a protective seal. The design can be the simple but powerful protection rune Elhaz or the ancient occult pentacle, which is the shape described by the beautiful planet Venus in her path around the heavens. Alternatively you could use the symbol of a hand. Once, people would use their own handprint as a protection or warning sign. There are minor chakras in the palms through which psychic energy can be both drawn and expelled, thus healers will 'lay on hands' to cure. It is also possible to direct energy into a palm print to protect a place or property.

Creating Your Own Duk Rak

Light a red candle and burn amber joss or incense. Find that still spot inside yourself, as in the exercise to quieten the mind (page 20). Breathing evenly, concentrate on what you are doing. Using the colour red, paint each stave or stone with your chosen design, being aware all the time that you are doing so with the intention of protecting your property. When this is done, take the seals along with the candle and incense and, starting at the main gate, walk steadily clockwise (sunwise) around your boundary. Firmly plant a seal design outwards at each corner and entrance as you go. The seals should be placed discreetly, or hidden if you wish.

As you place each seal, say, 'I place you here to protect all that I have and all that I love by earth, sky, fire and water, forever. *Le see kel. Le see kel. Le see kel.*'

As you walk, visualise a line of vibrant blue or rainbow fire following your footsteps and connecting each seal. Finish at your main entrance again, placing the last seal. Pause for a moment to visualise the line of blue fire encircling your property. It rises above your home and joins together to make a dome overhead. Enjoy the feeling of security for a moment, then consciously bring yourself back to the mundane world. Have a cup of tea and something to eat.

The wife of a long-distance truck driver from Sheffield was on the verge of a nervous breakdown. She was afraid to be alone at night, especially as they lived in an area of high crime. Her husband's long absences meant she rarely had a good night's sleep, usually spending the night on the living room sofa. After a week or two of

---

A similar exercise can be done at any time when you are feeling uneasy or before you go to sleep at night. Visualise the blue line of fire. In your mind's eye slowly draw its vibrant protective beam around yourself, your bed, or your property. Try to imagine every detail of its path until it finally closes in a protective circle. Alternatively draw a pentacle around yourself in the same way.

---

practising the above exercise she found herself able to sleep soundly for the first time in months; moreover, although neighbouring properties suffered break-ins, hers was never touched.

Magical Guardians

An ancient Gypsy protection for the home is a 'duk koor', a guardian spirit. Obtain a statuette that seems to embody the qualities you feel are needed to guard your home from evil and harm. It can be an animal – a dog or cat for instance – or have a human form – a warrior or a pagan deity. Some people have an angel or saint. It needn't be expensive, but it must be attractive to you and invoke a feeling of protection and confidence.

Imagine the spirit of the creature portrayed taking up residence in the statuette. Think of its personality, its likes and dislikes. Give it a name. Welcome it to your home, and set it in a suitable position. Tell it the reason it is there, and that you are confident in its powers. Make it little gifts, maybe flowers and incense. Every day before leaving home ask it to guard your property, and thank it for looking after it when you return. What you are doing is creating and charging a kind of battery to store and emit protective energy. The longer you do this the stronger the protection will become. You can also make a duk koor for your vehicle or garden.

Clearing Out Bad Luck

Sometimes people complain to me that since moving house, or some other occurrence in the past, they have had terrible luck. Nothing goes right. Disaster follows disaster. There is a simple but effective Romany ritual that clears away this kind of dark, bad luck and attracts good luck for the future. The best time to do this ritual is on the day of the new moon.

Sweeping Out Bad Luck

If you think deeply about the start of this period of bad luck you will find that there is some object that you acquired round about then or that you used or wore quite a lot. Maybe it is something that brings back recollections of an unhappy event. It can be an ornament, an item of clothing, or even a kitchen utensil.

Place the said object near the back door of the house. Then, using a broom, and starting at the top of the house or in the room furthest from the back door, sweep each room in turn, working in an anti-clockwise direction. As you work, visualise darkness being swept away in front of you. The darkness is black heavy clouds of bad luck. It can't resist your broom. While you sweep, say, 'I banish the dark clouds from my home, bad luck be gone, there is no place here for you. Be gone, be gone, be gone!'

Any dust can be swept on to a shovel and taken with you as you go. Do each room in turn until you reach the back door, then put all the sweepings into a bag outside. Take the object mentioned previously and break or tear it, venting all your anger and frustration. Put the pieces into the bag with the dust. Sprinkle the contents with salt, saying, 'By this salt, cleansing gift of the earth, I render you powerless.'

Now bury the bag. If it is at all possible, bury it at a crossroads or by running water, but if this is not practical bury it in the garden or at the bottom of the rubbish bin. Before covering the bag with earth, or rubbish, sprinkle it with salt, making a pattern of a cross within a circle, saying, 'By this salt, by this sign you are gone from my life.'

Now, reversing the order of the rooms, from the back door to the top of the house walk round each room clockwise with a lighted candle, preferably coloured pink or gold, and a lighted incense stick perfumed amber or rose. Alternatively, if there is a particular perfume that makes you feel happy, use that. As you walk, say, 'I bring light, joy, luck and love into every corner of my home and life!' Visualise each room being filled with bright golden light, every corner bursting with hope and joy. When you have done, return to the room most often used and leave the candle and incense to burn out naturally. Take time to enjoy the new feeling of happiness filling your home.

No matter how bad things seem, the wheel of life always turns. The longest spell of misfortune ends in time, but a little knowledge makes the wheel turn that much faster and helps to protect against the worst calamities.

Magic of the Planets

Using the right colours and doing the rites at the correct time on the best day can greatly increase the effectiveness of what you do. However, if this is not possible, don't be put off. Although the following list shows the colours generally used for different purposes, if you feel strongly attracted to a different colour at the time you wish to work a particular rite, this may be the colour you should be using.

Each day is ruled by a particular planet, for instance, the sun on Sunday, the moon on Monday, and so on, and each hour of the day is also ruled by a planet. So if, for instance, you wanted to dedicate a talisman for health, you would do it on Sunday, in an hour ruled by the sun.

Day	Planet	Rules	Colour
Sunday	Sun	Health, success, luck	Yellow, red, gold
Monday	Moon	Travel, magical working	Silver, white, violet
Tuesday	Mars	Military matters, fighting, discord	Red, orange, dark blue
Wednesday	Mercury	Study, inspiration, communication	Purple, yellow, light blue
Thursday	Jupiter	Luck, success, wealth, honour	Purple, gold, green, blue
Friday	Venus	Love, lust, beauty, friendship	Pink, green, red
Saturday	Saturn	Study, esoteric ideas, calmness	Black, indigo, light blue

Hours	Sunday	Monday	Tuesday	Wednesday	Thursday	Friday	Saturday
midnight–1 a.m	Sun	Moon	Mars	Mercury	Jupiter	Venus	Saturn
1–2 a.m.	Venus	Saturn	Sun	Moon	Mars	Mercury	Jupiter
2–3 a.m.	Mercury	Jupiter	Venus	Saturn	Sun	Moon	Mars
3–4 a.m.	Moon	Mars	Mercury	Jupiter	Venus	Saturn	Sun
4–5 a.m.	Saturn	Sun	Moon	Mars	Mercury	Jupiter	Venus
5–6 a.m.	Jupiter	Venus	Saturn	Sun	Moon	Mars	Mercury
6–7 a.m.	Mars	Mercury	Jupiter	Venus	Saturn	Sun	Moon
7–8 a.m.	Sun	Moon	Mars	Mercury	Jupiter	Venus	Saturn
8–9 a.m.	Venus	Saturn	Sun	Moon	Mars	Mercury	Jupiter
9–10 a.m.	Mercury	Jupiter	Venus	Saturn	Sun	Moon	Mars
10–11 a.m.	Moon	Mars	Mercury	Jupiter	Venus	Saturn	Sun
11 a.m.–noon	Saturn	Sun	Moon	Mars	Mercury	Jupiter	Venus
noon–1 p.m.	Jupiter	Venus	Saturn	Sun	Moon	Mars	Mercury
1–2 p.m.	Mars	Mercury	Jupiter	Venus	Saturn	Sun	Moon
2–3 p.m.	Sun	Moon	Mars	Mercury	Jupiter	Venus	Saturn
3–4 p.m.	Venus	Saturn	Sun	Moon	Mars	Mercury	Jupiter
4–5 p.m.	Mercury	Jupiter	Venus	Saturn	Sun	Moon	Mars
5–6 p.m.	Moon	Mars	Mercury	Jupiter	Venus	Saturn	Sun
6–7 p.m.	Saturn	Sun	Moon	Mars	Mercury	Jupiter	Venus
7–8 p.m.	Jupiter	Venus	Saturn	Sun	Moon	Mars	Mercury
8–9 p.m.	Mars	Mercury	Jupiter	Venus	Saturn	Sun	Moon
9–10 p.m.	Sun	Moon	Mars	Mercury	Jupiter	Venus	Saturn
10–11 p.m.	Venus	Saturn	Sun	Moon	Mars	Mercury	Jupiter
11 p.m.–midnight	Mercury	Jupiter	Venus	Saturn	Sun	Moon	Mars

Perfumes can be used as oils or incense. Incense can be loose, made of herbs and gums burned over charcoal, or it may be in the form of joss sticks or cones. Choose a perfume suited to the planet that rules your purpose, as in the above table, or one to which you are strongly attracted. Any perfume is better than none, unless you feel that is strikes a discordant note.

Planet	Perfume
Sun	Heliotrope, marigold, sunflower, myrrh, frankincense, sandalwood
Moon	Amber, sandalwood, night queen, jasmine, poppy, church incense
Mars	Benzoin, geranium, cedarwood, cinnamon
Mercury	Sandalwood, marjoram, benzoin, mystic herb
Jupiter	Sandalwood, benzoin, frankincense, myrrh, patchouli
Venus	Rose, violet, musk, jasmine, ylang-ylang
Saturn	Myrrh, musk, cypress, church incense

Special Symbols

Icelandic rune-based talismans are still very popular today. Though not widely used by the Gypsy people of this country, my granny thought that they were some of the most powerful symbols she had used. They are best painted in red on slivers of fruit wood, and dedicated with the help of Odin, Lord of the Runes. Incidentally, I have noticed lately that many banks and other businesses are incorporating rune signs into their logos, whether by accident or design I don't know.

This is a symbol to attract success and to make your dreams come true. To have your wish granted, hold this charm in your left hand while you make the wish. Then bury it at the foot of a fruit tree.

Use this symbol to attract love. It will also make those you need to impress well disposed towards you.

This is a powerful symbol for attracting prosperity. Keep this one in your purse or pocket and it will never be empty.

Put this one under your pillow, hang it over your bed or wear it round your neck to heal mental and physical sickness.

The cornucopia, or horn of plenty, is another ancient and powerful symbol; associated with Isis Furtuna, it attracts all kinds of wealth and luck. The Gypsies often used to wear a cornucopia of gold or silver round the neck on a chain. This symbol of the Earth Mother will ensure you have all that you need when you need it. Horn-shaped seashells are another form of the cornucopia, and considered lucky for the same reason.

Perhaps the most well known of all the Cabalistic talismans, the pentacle of Solomon is used for attracting all good things into your life and clearing away obstructions. It is also helpful to those who wish to practise magic, and should be worn by anyone engaged in communication with the spirit world to protect them from harmful influences.

The eye is a very ancient symbol, used for protection and to avert evil. It is well known to the Gypsy people and used to be painted on the horse's harness. Commonly used in ancient Egypt as the all-seeing protective eye of Horus, it can still be seen protecting the small fishing vessels of the Mediterranean.

Despite its unfortunate associations with the Nazis, the swastika is an Icelandic symbol and world-wide sign that dates back to prehistoric times, when it was used for all kinds of protection. It is also a symbol of progress and rebirth.

The cup or chalice is a universal symbol of love and spirituality. The design illustrated is a Gypsy talisman to attract true and lasting love. It is especially effective if drawn on pink paper, or silk, scented with a drop of rose oil, and worn close to the heart. If there is someone special you wish to attract, make two talismans at the same time from the same material and hide the second one where the object of your affection will sit or stand when in your presence.

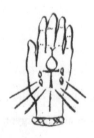

This is a Gypsy talisman for good health, possibly based on the Egyptian ankh. The snake has only recently become associated with evil, and in most cultures the world over the snake was venerated as a sign of wisdom and healing. Even today the badge of the medical profession is the caduceus, two snakes twined round a winged rod. This is also the badge of Hermes, or Mercury, the god of wisdom.

Fortune-Telling Through Dreams and Tea Leaves

The ability to foretell events is a useful talent. Early man consulted his shaman about the following day's hunt, and kings and generals employed their own seers for advice on affairs of state, marriages and wars. The stars of entertainment, business tycoons, even politicians consult with astrologers, Tarot-readers or other psychics before making important decisions.

The methods men have used to predict the future have been as many and as varied as the leaves on the trees. The strange thing is that once the ground rules governing each method of prediction have been established the oracle will obligingly obey these rules. The bird will fly, the pendulum will swing, the stones will fall, the cards will be dealt in precisely the right way to tell the true story of things to come.

The shape of a cloud, the flight of a bird, dreams, runes, tea leaves, palmistry, crystal-gazing, astrology, dice, cards, eggs, water, fire, sand, the surface of a drum, the seeds in a fruit, sticks, stones, even the twitching entrails of newly dispatched sacrificial victims, both animal and human: the list of ways and means used for divination goes on and on, only limited by man's imagination and ingenuity. But just as a candle needs a match to set it alight, so the oracle needs the spark of psychic understanding to bring to light the full meaning behind the signs and omens.

Fortune-telling is probably the art most closely associated with the Gypsy people, and the Romanies have been familiar with most of the above methods of prediction at one time or another (except for the steaming entrails, of course). Perhaps the most familiar methods of prediction nowadays are the Tarot, the crystal ball and palmistry, but there are many other oracles that have been widely used by the Romanies through the years.

Two that spring to mind involve a tambourine, or a simple hand drum. One method involves throwing beans, grains of corn or small stones on to a drum that is marked into sections; the fortune is told by noting into which section the beans fall. In the other method a question is asked and all the possible answers are given while the drum skin is rubbed in a circular motion. When the enquirer reaches the correct answer the fingers will stick to the surface of the drum. Interestingly, a similar principle is used in radeathesia, an alternative medical therapy sometimes known as 'the black box'. Simply put, this uses a machine with a diaphragm that is rubbed while the practitioner turns labelled dials. The practitioner's finger sticks to the diaphragm when the correct diagnosis and treatment are 'dialled in'.

Another method of prediction that I believe is still widely used by Gypsies on the Continent has the client shaking a number of beans in their hand, along with a coin that they provide. The fortune is told from the position of the beans on the palm when the hand is opened. Of course, the coin is collected as payment when the beans are returned to the Gypsy's pocket.

Lancashire Romanies would often drop the white of an egg into a glass of water, making their predictions from the patterns thus revealed. For a yes or no answer to a question they would improvise a pendulum with a ring hung from a thread or hair. This method was also used with success to predict the sex of an unborn child.

One strange little quirk of human nature that I have noticed over the years is that many people will quite happily pay good money to be told a lot of nonsense about tall dark strangers, unexpected windfalls and bungalows by the sea, but become frightened and refuse to have their fortune told again when the prediction proves true and has real bearing on their life and situation. Not long ago, a regular client brought a friend along for a reading who is reported to have said, 'I'm not going to her again, it's too weird. Everything she said came true!'

I suppose this attitude springs from the fear of being told something terrible, though in reality tragedy and death are rare occurrences in the lives of most people, and can sometimes be avoided by being forewarned. I know that some fortune-tellers, particularly certain fairground ladies, take satisfaction in pronouncing gloom, doom and death for one and all. Several times I have had to try to repair the needless damage caused to the peace of mind of my clients by these thoughtless people. A reputable psychic would not be so careless of people's feelings.

Of course there are times of sadness in everyone's life, and death is inevitable in the end – but the future is not fixed. Never listen to someone who tells you authoritatively that something will definitely happen no matter what steps you might take to avoid it. Although our karma dictates the lessons we need to learn in this life, thus providing us with the map we have to follow, we all have a certain control over our destiny. We are free to choose which road to take on our own given map; otherwise, life would be pointless.

All methods of prediction rely on the insight of the seer, the spark of intuition that is in each and every one of us. Intuition, the predictive zee energy, was once essential for survival in primitive man, but is now for the most part buried so deeply in modern man that it is scorned as a myth.

Whatever method of prediction you choose, the basic preparatory steps are the same; earlier chapters show you how to get in touch with your own zee energy. Find the quiet spot inside yourself as before (page 20). Take several deep breaths, feel the zee energy enter your body with each breath. Take it right down into your stomach, then lift it up into the throat and head area to awaken the chakras there. Feel your thoughts quieten, and say a little prayer for guidance, then concentrate on the method in hand.

It is useful, of course, to learn the symbols associated with each method of prediction, but these are just guidelines. Sometimes you will find that different authorities will give different interpretations of the same symbol; nothing is written in tablets of stone. You will find a story comes to mind inspired by the method you are using – just say what comes to mind. All it takes is a little confidence. The more you practise, the greater your

> Fortune-telling provides a tool that can help us choose
> the correct road, point out the pitfalls or predict a
> happier time, the sunshine at the seemingly endless
> tunnel of despair, thus giving us the heart to carry
> on when things seem hopeless.

confidence will become as you realise your ability. Just try, you will surprise yourself.

One little word of caution: although I have never known a prediction to be false, I have known things to come about in a perverse and unexpected manner. The reading may be literally true but quite different from the result expected at the time. Remember the old tale about the man who was happy to be told that he wouldn't die until snow fell in summer, but was then killed one bright sunny day by a horse called Snow who fell on top of him. The story may be fiction but it serves to illustrate my point.

And please, please remember that fortune-telling is not a game and should never be undertaken lightly. If you decide to read for others you are taking on a great responsibility. A careless word can cause months of anxiety and even adversely change the course of someone's life. Be sure of your motives. A desire to impress is not a good reason to tell someone's fortune, nor is the desire to 'put someone down' or frighten him or her. If, however, you feel confident in your abilities there is nothing wrong in charging for a reading. Few people nowadays value something they don't have to pay for, and a good reading should be valued.

Dreams

The world of dreams is a strange and fascinating place. Philosophers have hypothesised that the waking world is all a dream, and dreams the reality, while psychologists tell us that we need to dream to keep us sane. Even animals dream. Sometimes our dogs act in a very guilty manner when they first awaken, and other times they seem relieved to see us. Perhaps they have been dreaming that they were naughty, or lost. Most dreams are muddled fantasy versions of everyday life, incorporating actual events with things we may have read about or seen on TV as well as those things that are uppermost in our minds at the moment.

Other dreams are especially vivid, and they sometimes stay with us for weeks. Our subconscious tells us there is something out of the ordinary, even portentous, about such dreams. Quite often the dream is about a problem that one doesn't want to admit to, making itself felt in symbolic form.

A young man came to see me troubled by a recurring nightmare. He dreamed that he was on the shores of a beautiful lake whose water was crystal clear and inviting. He couldn't wait to dive in. Throwing off his clothes, he dived headfirst into the clear water, but suddenly it was a thick muddy slime from which he couldn't escape, no matter how he struggled. He felt himself drowning, and that is where the dream ended.

I knew this man had been married for only two years. Both he and his wife were romantic, idealistic and very much in love. They had one child, just over a year old, and his wife was pregnant again. A self-employed person, the man had been used to picking and choosing what work he would do, but now had to earn a more regular income.

It was obvious to me that the dream was a metaphor for his life. The clear lake was the marriage into which he had plunged so happily. The slime in which he was drowning was the morass of responsibility in which he found himself unexpectedly embroiled. In his waking life he admitted to nothing but happiness in his situation, but his dream showed his inner worry at having to provide for a family. A dream like this tells us that it is impossible to lie to ourselves, no matter how hard we try. Only by confronting our worries can we work out a solution.

It is unusual, though, for a dream to be so clear. Most predictive dreams take the form of symbols. We wake up knowing that there was something significant about the bird or cat in our dream, but can't think why it should be so. It was for this reason that great leaders of the past employed seers to interpret their dreams. The

Man has always known that some dreams are augurs of the future. There are rare occasions when a dream is a straightforward prediction of events to come. One night I had a very vivid dream. I was in the van driving to work with my husband. Suddenly he said, 'Oh – oh! Something's wrong, the brakes have gone!' Thick black smoke filled the cab, and the engine burst into flames.

I couldn't escape from my seatbelt and became overcome with smoke.

The next morning, as we actually were driving to work, events unfolded exactly as they had done in my dream, but because the dream had made me think of what I would do in such an emergency we were able to rescue ourselves, our dogs, and our most important possessions without panic before the van was engulfed in flames.

Romany people set great store by dreams, and are not embarrassed to discuss them openly if the meaning seems obscure.

It would take a whole book to cover all the possible symbols and interpretations found in dreams, so I have picked out the most common and important in Romany lore. Sometimes two or more symbols will appear in the same dream, in which case they should be considered together to make a story. For instance, an axe, bird and fruit all in the same dream might mean that now is the time to push yourself forward and use your initiative at work. If you do your life will take a turn for the better, bringing promotion and financial gain.

Romany Dream Lore

ACCIDENT To be involved in an accident: take care whom you trust. To watch an accident happen: someone close to you is in trouble.

ANGEL Someone loves you. You will be protected from harm.

ANIMALS Domestic animals: happiness, true friends. Wild animals: a friend is angry with you. An animal chasing you, someone is jealous. Lambs or young animals playing: an addition to the family. Lion or other big cat: power and promotion.

ANTS Work will keep you busy, but will bring rewards.

ARROW You will be let down by someone you trust.

AXE Stick up for yourself. You will get your own way.

BABY A sign of happiness to come. A new way of life is open to you.

BASKET OR BAG If full: you are carrying too much worry or responsibility. If empty: you will suffer a loss.

BAT Flying near you: a false friend. Away from you: unseen danger.

BEES A very fortunate omen, life will be good.

BIRDS Your life will soon improve. Lark or other songbird: great happiness. Owl, silently looking: lessons learned. Owl hooting mournfully or cock crowing: your sins will find you out.

BOAT A change of abode. If the water is calm: the change will be for the better. If stormy: things will not go smoothly.

BOOK If you are reading a book, you will make a discovery. If the book is closed, you are turning a blind eye to something.

BRIDGE A needless worry will soon be resolved.

BUTTERFLY An unfaithful lover.

CAGE Loss of freedom, others rely on you.

CARAVAN A long journey.

CASTLE A dream fulfilled brings responsibility.

CHILDREN Playing: a happy marriage. Crying children: delayed marriage.

CHURCH OR CHAPEL A bad sign: be careful in what you say or do. A church service: worry about relatives or close friends.

CORN Prosperity.

DAGGER If you are threatened: an enemy is waiting to hurt you. If you hold the dagger: you bring trouble upon yourself.

DEATH Death and all things connected to it: a new start.

DEVIL Your baser instincts take over; try to avoid temptation.

DRINK If you are drinking: you need more out of life. If you are drunk: you will be successful, but don't let it go to your head.

DRUMS Bad news.

EGGS Unbroken: gain. Broken: loss.

FIRE Things get out of hand.

FISHING Ambitions realised. Fish jumping: when opportunity comes your way, be ready.

FOG OR MIST If you are lost in a mist, things don't turn out quite as you expect.

FRUIT Prosperity. Rotten fruit: you will not gain as much as you hoped. Apple: love. A bad apple: love will not bring you joy.

HARVEST To reap corn, or harvest fruit and vegetables: you will reap the fruits of your labour.

HILLS To climb up: you will gain recognition. To descend: a disappointment. (The same interpretations apply to ladders, stairs or any climbing dream.) To look down over the edge of a precipice: be cautious or disaster may strike.

HORSESHOE Luck in gambling. A horse: someone wishes to help you; good advice comes your way.

ICE, SNOW, HAIL Failure and dispute.

INVISIBILITY If you are invisible: you feel that you are not getting enough attention; don't make a fool of yourself. If someone else is invisible: they need your help; don't ignore them.

JEALOUSY You are feeling insecure.

JEWELLERY You will become rich.

KEY Marriage.

KNIFE Illness.

LAMP If the lamp is lit: you are intelligent, and able to see the truth. If unlit: you need more mental stimulation.

LEAVES AND TREES A good omen for growth in all areas of
life. A new friendship is in the air. Health improves. Laurel
leaves: success and fame. A garden bonfire: loss and sadness in
the family.

LETTER Urgent news.

LIGHTNING Success in an unexpected manner.

LOVE OR ABSENT FRIEND If they are sad: they miss you. If
happy: they don't really care.

MOON Happiness, especially in love.

NEST If the nest has eggs or chicks: home and family bring
happiness. If the nest is empty: sadness in the home; you pine
for someone.

NUDITY You make a grave mistake.

PAINTING AND DECORATING A false friend; you see through
them but pretend not to. A situation is not to your liking but
you put up with it for the sake of peace.

PURSE An empty purse is a good omen. A full purse: theft.

QUICKSAND OR MUD A lucky dream, meaning social
advancement, a fortunate marriage.

RAIN Trouble at home or work.

RAINBOW Good health. A dream comes true.

RING Marriage.

RUNNING Enthusiasm could overcome your better judgement.

SPIDER Money comes unexpectedly.

STARS In the sky: success through friends. Falling stars: failure,
discord.

STEALING If you are the thief: you will overcome an enemy or rival. If you are stolen from: a small gain comes your way.

STONES Sorrow or bad health.

STRAW Loss of money.

SUN To be in the sun: a worry will be relieved. If the sun comes from behind a cloud: you will learn the truth about something that has puzzled you.

TENT To be inside a tent: security and peace of mind. To erect a tent: you lay good groundwork for the future.

TUNNEL A change of abode. Excitement, new experiences.

WATCHES AND CLOCKS You lack independence. Disappointing employment prospects; you don't like your work.

WITCH OR WIZARD You may gain through creativity or imagination.

WORMS A storm in a teacup. You are letting trivialities get on top of you.

WOUNDS, CUTS, BRUISES AND ILLNESS Love comes unexpectedly. Hasty marriage.

Reading the Tea Leaves

Now that most people use teabags in preference to loose tea, the art of teacup-reading has become neglected, which is a pity because I have known even the most complete novice to make remarkably accurate predictions using this method.

In the old days, a Romany woman would read a housewife's tea leaves in exchange for a refreshing cuppa and a few old clothes. Sometimes a Gypsy Queen, dressed in her finest and laden with all her jewellery, would preside over a special tea-drinking party for a few favoured clients. The best bone china and lace tablecloth would be brought out to impress upon the Rawnies (ladies) the importance of the occasion – and how privileged they were to be invited. No doubt the fee for the teacup-reading was suitably increased to fit the occasion.

It is not only tea leaves that can be used for this type of reading: coffee and cocoa grounds, or anything that leaves a sediment in the cup, can be used in the same way. If you prefer teabags, you can of course break open the bag before making the tea in the usual way. This should ensure that a good pattern is left in the cup, but if you do take the trouble to make a good old-fashioned pot of loose-leafed tea, you will also have the extra bonus of a truly satisfying taste.

One drawback I find with reading the teacups is that it is all too easy to fall into the habit of reading the cups at every tea break, which tends to belittle this method and turn it into a parlour game. But as long as it is used with respect it will give excellent results.

Most authorities state that the cup should be plain white and shallow, but I have never found that the shape of the cup was important, nor that a patterned cup adversely affected the reading. Indeed, Romanies have always dislike plain white china, preferring it to be richly decorated.

How to Read Tea Leaves

The enquirer should drink their tea until only a spoonful or so is left in the bottom of the cup. They should hold the cup in the left hand and swirl it around three times in an anti-clockwise direction, then turn it upside down to drain. The cup is then passed to the person who is to read it.

Prepare to do the reading by quietening the mind (page 20). Hold the cup with the handle in your right hand, or you can hold it in both hands if it feels more comfortable. The brain likes to make pictures out of abstract blobs, which is why we see faces in stained walls or castles in clouds. It is this principle that inspires the psyche to see omens in the tea leaves. Move the cup about if it helps you to see the patterns clearly. It can also help if you let your eyes go slightly out of focus.

The leaves should be read in a kind of spiral motion working anti-clockwise from the handle around the rim, back to the handle, then the sides, and finally the bottom of the cup. As a general rule, the nearer to the rim of the cup a symbol appears, the sooner the event will take place. The further down the cup, the further into the future it will be. The larger the symbol, the greater will be the impact on the enquirer's life.

Signs in the Cup

Numerals are usually time factors, for instance, three days, three weeks, three months, depending on where they appear in the cup, though in the case of one lucky client the large-figure three surrounded by dots stood for the three thousand pounds he won on the lottery. Letters are usually the initials of a person or place.

There are times when the leaves make a picture that is an obvious illustration of an event, such as two people fighting, a wedding, a baby or an accident, and your intuition will tell you that this is exactly how it should be read. At other times the pattern may be of unconnected symbols, or several symbols close together, which should be read as a whole. For instance, a nail, a ring and a rose taken together would show that a spiteful person might try to come between you and your lover, but that yours is a true and lasting affection that will overcome adversity. If as you watch a picture is changed by the shifting of a leaf, read the two symbols as a story; for example, a horseshoe changing to the letter L could mean luck through someone whose name begins with L.

The following is a list of the signs most commonly found in the teacups.

ACORN Good luck, especially if starting a new enterprise.
AEROPLANE A journey. Take care; there is danger of an accident. A crashing plane: be careful in business. Hopes are unfulfilled.
ANCHOR A lucky symbol bringing stability in your affairs.
ANGEL Protection, love, good news.
ANIMALS Domestic animals: friends. Domestic animals snarling: friends turn on you or behave strangely. Wild animals: a new experience, independence. Wild animals attacking: beware of enemies.
ANT Success through hard work.
ANVIL Others rely on you, and may expect too much. Don't be taken for granted.

APPLE You learn something to your advantage. For the student, the chance of further education.

ARROW Hasty news, probably bad.

AXE Difficulties overcome.

BAG A journey. Basket, material gain.

BALL OR BALLOON You have little control over your own life.

BAT Friends talk behind your back.

BEE A lucky few months to come. Things go your way.

BELL Unexpected good news about family or close friends.

BIRDS A letter brings good news. If it is an owl: be wise, keep your own council.

BOAT Help in time of trouble.

BOOK You will have dealings with the law, solicitors or some official body.

BOOT Generally a lucky sign. You will move on in life. A planned journey will be a happy one. Difficulties pass.

BOTTLE Don't neglect health problems.

BOUQUET OR FLOWERS Very lucky; true love, true friends, happiness in all areas of life.

BOW You will gain what you hope for, but only through hard work.

BRIDGE An excellent opportunity is given to you.

BROOM OR BRUSH You can sweep all your worries away.

BUTTERFLY A care-free period is about to begin.

CAGE Restriction. Illness.

CANDLE You can be of help to others.

CASTLE Promotion. Official position.

CHAIN Marriage or business contract. Broken chain: unhappy marriage, a broken or unwise contract.

CHAIR Happiness in domestic matters. Security, contentment.

CHURCH Marriage, christening or funeral, depending on surrounding omens.

CIRCLE Completion of any matter concerning the enquirer at the time.

CLOVER Good luck. Four-leafed clover: exceptional luck.

COFFIN The end of something.

CORN Prosperity; money worries end.

CROOK A shepherd's crook, others rely on you to take the lead. Your advice is requested.

CROSS Sacrifice, unhappiness.

CROWN Success.

CUP Your efforts are noticed and rewarded.

DAGGER An enemy tries to harm you.

DEVIL You feel like letting your hair down. Don't overdo it; you may suffer.

DOTS Money.

EAR Take no notice of gossip.

EYE Be aware of what is going on around you.

FACE A new friendship, or an old friend comes back into your life. If the face is unpleasant, beware; the person is not as nice as they seem.

FAN Don't try to cover up the truth; it will cause trouble in the future.

FEATHER Something you laugh at may not be so trivial after all.

FENCE Obstacles.

FIST Something threatens you. Quarrels and disputes.

FOOT A journey overseas.

GALLOWS A loss of money or position.

GUN Someone speaks ill of you.

HAT OR HELMET You are offered work.

HEART Love, marriage.

HORSESHOE Good luck in all these things.

HOURGLASS You may not have as much time to finish a task as you expect. Do it now.

HOUSE Home, family, security. Help from the family.

INSECTS Minor worries and irritations.

IVY Faithful lovers and friends.

JUG Good health.

KETTLE Contentment in the home.

KEY New project. The future is in your hands.

KNIFE Separation, broken friendship, or love affair.

LADDER Advancement.

LAMP The lamp throws light on something that has puzzled you. The way ahead is clear.

LEAVES AND TREES Good news, good health, growth.

LETTER News is on the way.

LIGHTHOUSE Take heed of any warning given to you.

LINES Movement. Single line: advancement. Double lines: a journey. Long lines that cross: decisions that affect the course of your life.

MERMAID Temptation.

MOON A new moon: good fortune, especially for new ventures. Half-moon: love. Old moon: bad luck.

MUSICAL INSTRUMENTS Peace, harmony.

NAIL Enemies try to harm you. Two-faced friends.

NET Beware pitfalls. Danger surrounds you.

PICKAXE Determination gets you what you want.

PEOPLE Representations of people mean exactly what they show, for instance, a policeman, an old woman, a doctor, or someone angry, sad, celebrating, and so on.

PYRAMID Concentrate on the spiritual side of life.

QUESTION MARK Indecision. The symbols around it should help to make up your mind.

RAINBOW Hope for the future. End of strife.

RING True and lasting love.

SADDLE Take advantage of any opportunity that comes your way.

SCALES You will be treated just as you deserve. If the scales are weighed down at one side: you will be unjustly treated. If they are weighed down with a lucky symbol close by: you will get away with something or get off lightly.

SCYTHE The sudden end of something. Accident. Death.

SHELL Good news, happiness near water.

SHIPWRECK Theft. Loss. Forlorn hope.

SKULL A warning sign. Danger. Avoid risk. Death.

SNAKE Recovery from illness.

SPADE A period of hard work.

SPIDER Persistence will pay off.

SPOON Others prove helpful.

STAR Good fortune. Shooting star, sudden fame.

SUN Happiness, confidence.

TABLE A gathering, a party.

TEAPOT A small gathering. Don't speak ill of others.

TENT An adventurous period in your life. A new job may find you doing something completely different.

TRIANGLE Pointing upwards: success. Pointing downwards: failure.

TRIDENT Prongs upwards: gain through the sea, a journey by water, a sailor comes into your life. Prongs downwards: loss through water.

UMBRELLA Protection. Help comes when needed.

VOLCANO Something kept hidden suddenly emerges. Anger. Frustration.

WAGON Inheritance.

WHEEL A turning point in life.

Natural Signs and Omens, Including Weather Lore

Living a life that made them acutely aware of the natural world, our ancestors noticed that some animals were more special than others, wiser, craftier or touched with an aura that seemed to light up the space around. Some seemed to embody the characteristics of certain gods, and became symbols of, or messengers for, those deities. In the plant world too, some species were looked on with special reverence, perhaps because of their healing, narcotic or toxic properties. It could be the shape of the leaves or root, or in the case of trees their magnificent appearance and great age.

The sky was a ceaseless source of wonder, the home of the gods, full of signs and portents for those with eyes to see and the knowledge to interpret the meaning of the awesome panorama above.

It wasn't strange that people who saw nature as the work of the gods, and themselves as part of it, should find meaning and auguries in the things around them. Omens were drawn from unnatural events of all kinds, but special note was taken of anything involving those things considered sacred to the gods.

The great civilisations of the ancient world made this kind of divination into a fine art, and natural omens were used to help decide the fate of nations. Today natural omens are considered by most people to be the remnants of superstition. However, if you follow what has been said previously about prayers and putting your faith in God, natural omens can provide both warning and guidance. This doesn't mean that every time you see a crow or other special creature it has a meaning, but if you are looking for help in making a decision and one appears, or if at any time one should make its presence felt in no uncertain way, then this should be taken as significant.

Although there is a general consensus about the meanings of most omens, there are times when people disagree as to whether a thing is good or bad depending on their own personal mindset and the happy or sad associations it may bring. Even among the Romanies, some families may consider a thing lucky while to others it would be unlucky, or the same creature bring good or bad news according to its behaviour. As with most things in the occult world, you should trust your own instincts. The overwhelming feeling of good or ill will tell you if the omen is good or bad. The following list of natural omens is by no means comprehensive, but they are the ones most likely to be encountered in your daily life. The meanings given are the ones I find to be true.

Birds

Birds have a great deal of lore associated with them. Being able to fly between heaven and earth, birds are natural messengers of the gods. If a wild bird of any kind should alight on a person, that person is destined for fame, and we have all heard the phrase 'muck for luck': bird droppings on yourself or your property bring luck within a week.

Romanies love birds. Many keep fancy game fowl and 'banties' (or bantams). Children often own their own cockerels, which they are allowed to sell or exchange as they wish. The children are taught to be responsible and look after their own birds, taking great pride in the condition of their pets.

COCKERELS AND DOVES Cockerels are prominent in folk tradition, sounding a warning or reproaching the guilty. A cockerel crowing in the night brings bad news the next day. If a cockerel should crow on the afternoon of a wedding day in the hearing of the happy couple, it foretells an unhappy and quarrelsome marriage, and if a cockerel should stand in the bride's path and crow complete disaster is forecast. On the other hand, if the newly married pair should come across a pair of cooing doves, the marriage will be long and happy.

CROWS All members of the crow family are surrounded by mystery. Considered to be exceptionally wise and intelligent, some country people say that crows can live to be three hundred years old. The god Odin has two ravens associated with him, and Noah sent a raven out from the ark after the flood. To see one crow is said to bring sorrow, while two mean joy, but I have always been pleased to see any number of crows, finding it is the behaviour of the birds which is significant, not how many there are. A crow standing in the road signifies a happy journey to me, whilst a dead crow, a lucky omen to some, would cause me to turn back.

ROOKS To have property with a rookery on it, or in sight, is very fortunate, as long as the colony is fruitful. But if the rooks should desert the rookery, disaster and death are predicted. I once worked on an orchard with a thriving rookery near the main house. One morning the rookery was deserted; within a week the head of the family was dead. It is inviting disaster to shoot rooks. A Lincolnshire businessman laughed at this 'superstition' when he destroyed a colony on his property, but found himself bankrupt within a year and finally shot himself with the very gun he had used on the rooks. In Ireland, when one was buying a property that was blessed with a rookery the deal was once considered null and void if the rooks deserted the rookery within a year of the sale.

MAGPIES Magpies, also members of the crow family, are a sign of good luck if two are seen together, but one chattering near your property could be a warning of theft. This probably arises from the magpies' love of bright objects, which they will often collect to decorate their nests. My mother-in-law lost a treasured diamond engagement ring, and thought it was gone for good until boys playing in trees found it among bits of glass and other shiny things in the remains of a magpie's nest.

ROBINS AND WRENS The robin and the wren are both lucky creatures. They bring good news if they fly into your home, but a dead wren or robin near your door warns of bad news on the way.

OWLS An owl is often considered to be a bird of ill omen, and to hear an owl foretells bad news, but personally I love to hear the owls at night and find comfort in their nearness. Owls are a symbol of wisdom and often associated with goddess figures in different cultures. However to kill an owl is very bad luck, as is seeing one hunting in the daylight hours during winter, which foretells a time of need. But this is not true in the long summer days, when the owl needs to feed its family and the hours of darkness are short.

SWALLOWS   It is a fortunate house that has swallows nesting under the eaves. Good fortune will abide within. But if you destroy the nests and kill the birds, all happiness will fly away with them. As a child I often used to go along a country lane at Helsby near Chester, where a row of tiny cottages was blessed with so many generations of swallows' nests that they seemed to reach halfway down the walls. Whenever I see russet apples I am reminded of the friendly, smiling faces of the old people who lived there. It was said that they were the healthiest people for a hundred miles.

Animals

Animals too have their own large fund of lore.

CATS AND DOGS   If a black cat should cross your path it brings good luck. If the cat stops to look at you the luck will be greater, but if the cat spits at you it brings bad luck. Dogs howling for no apparent reason brings news of death.

FOXES   If a fox crosses your path, an opportunity will be given to you. If the fox stops to look at you, your most ambitious plans will come to fruition, but if the fox just glances disdainfully and walks away with his back to you, your plans will come to nothing.

HORSES   A white horse was once the symbol of the Celtic goddess Epona, and thus should be greeted with respect or you may draw down misfortune upon yourself, but you can tell the horse your hopes and wishes to make them come true.

STOATS AND WEASELS   Stoats and weasels are looked upon as bad luck by some Gypsy families, who would be horrified if one crossed their path. However, to others, including my own family, they are good luck. To see these delightful creatures playing means happiness in family matters, but if they should be squabbling family disputes will arise.

HARES   Hares are dedicated to the earth goddess. It is said that Boadicea carried a hare beneath her cloak to her first engagement with the Roman army. When she released the hare, it ran straight towards the Roman lines, leading the Celts to a great victory. To see a hare is a lucky thing. If you see one when you are on the way to an interview or meeting of any kind, a successful outcome is guaranteed.

FISH   The fish is a lucky symbol in most cultures. In myth and folklore, fish are often guardians of secrets and wisdom. To see a fish jump unexpectedly brings luck; if something is worrying you at the time, your worries are unfounded, and anything you are hoping for will be yours.

Insects

The insect world has its own signs and portents.

SPIDERS   Spiders have long held a fascination for man, and one should never kill a spider. If a spider should attach a filament of web to you, the fates are about to make a change in your life, or, as my dad would say, 'You've stood still too long!' A money spider should be allowed to have a good crawl all over you, before being gently and safely removed, to ensure that the luck 'sticks'.

CRANE-FLIES   A crane-fly or daddy-long-legs brings luck with it when it flies indoors, and should never be killed.

LADYBIRDS AND OTHER BEETLES   The ladybird is one of the most familiar and most loved insects: a seven-spotted ladybird brings luck when it lands on you. A beetle trundling across your path means a lucky day. The bigger the beetle, the greater the luck, so don't squash it.

BUTTERFLIES   A butterfly settling upon a young woman foretells a pregnancy; on an older woman it signifies a new baby in the family. On anyone else the butterfly foretells a time of celebration and frivolity.

Other Omens

THE MOON   To see the new moon out of doors is very lucky. You should bow to her three times, then turn your money over three times; it will increase ninefold by the next new moon. Make a wish on the full moon, and of course you should always wish on a shooting star – but never tell your wish to another, or it loses its power and won't come true.

OAK TREES AND BRAMBLES   The oak tree is lucky for money and health. Try to catch a falling oak leaf in autumn, before it touches the ground. Keep the leaf safely in your purse or wallet to ensure it will never be empty. If an oak leaf accidentally catches you on your person, this is very lucky and you should keep it safe. Likewise, if a bramble catches on your clothes it is considered lucky.

BEAN PLANTS   To find a lone bean plant growing in the wild is lucky, but never sleep or even stay too long near a bean patch in flower – the perfume can cause depression.

FLOWERS   Don't walk over a flower or a spray of leaves lost in the street. Rescue them, and put them in water for luck. To be given a bunch of flowers is to be given happiness.

ITCHING   If your left hand itches, money is coming. If the right hand itches, it is going. The right foot itching foretells a journey to a familiar place, while the left foot itching means the journey will be on strange ground. If your nose itches, expect a quarrel. If the left ear itches or burns, someone is speaking well of you. The right ear means spiteful gossip.

JOURNEYS   If you put your shoe on the wrong foot, or if a shoe strap breaks, forget any journey or new enterprise planned for that day. Likewise, if a Romany meets a funeral at the beginning of a journey, they will turn back, for nothing good will come of it. If, however, you accidentally take the wrong turn on a journey, continue that way if possible, as you may be avoiding trouble or meeting luck.

CLOTHING   It is a lucky sign if you accidentally put on a garment inside out. You should leave it that way until you have a legitimate reason to change it or you will reverse the luck. But if you should become elf-mazed – in other words, confused or lost, or lose something you have just put down – turn a garment inside out in order to break the spell.

FIRE   Sitting around the fire as Romanies do, they see many things in the flames. If the flame burns green, there will be news of a birth. If the flames are blue, an old person may be dying and wish to say goodbye. If the fire burns bright and clear in the evening, a lucky day will follow. If the wood sparks and crackles loudly, the fire should be given a good kick to ward off the dispute it is warning you about.

HORSESHOES   The horseshoe has long been a symbol of good fortune, so of course it is lucky to find one, but any piece of old iron found on a road or field can bring luck. Hold it in your right hand while you make a wish, then spit on it and throw it over your left shoulder. Walk on without looking where it has landed, though it is a good idea to make sure no one is standing behind you before you throw it!

The Weather

Of course, the fate of the nations, or even their own ultimate destiny, is not always the thing uppermost in the mind of people. It is quite likely to be something more mundane, like the weather. Weathermen will tell you that meteorology is a science nowadays, but it is sometimes a remarkably inaccurate one. If I was as wrong when reading the Tarot as often as the weather forecast seems to be, I would be out of business in no time. Some years ago a country weather prophet, famous for the accuracy of his predictions, was retiring. When asked for the secret of his success, he replied, 'I just sees what that idiot on TV says, then I says the opposite ...' It is no wonder that the Romanies still like to watch the natural weather forecast.

When you spend most of your life outdoors, it is handy to have some idea of what the weather is going to do. One tends to notice little differences: the smell of the air, the feel of the breeze. That betokens a change. All of creation, apart from man, seems to be sensitive to changing weather patterns. We seem to have lost this ability along with our other psychic senses during the process of civilisation (although those pour souls who suffer from any kind of rheumatism will tell you that they can certainly feel it in their bones). However, we can all observe nature, and note the indications of change in the world about us.

CLOUDS 'Red sky at night, sailor's delight. Red sky in morning, sailor's warning.' This little rhyme is chanted, with slight variations, all over the country, and with good reason, as it usually proves true. A mackerel sky predicts a fine day on the morrow, as long as the clouds are fine and high, but if the clouds are low, heavy or moving swiftly, wind can be expected. A greenish tinge in the evening sky shows rain on the way. If it is already raining and the clouds take on a greenish or lurid red hue, the rain will become heavier and be prolonged. However if a patch of blue appears and becomes larger as you watch, the rain is likely to clear within an hour. My mother used to call this 'a patch of blue for a sailor's trousers'. I have also heard it referred to as 'a patch of blue for a lady's cloak'.

Another little saying that usually proves true is 'Rain before seven, fine before eleven'. If the rain doesn't clear in this time it will probably last for several days.

THE MOON   If the sun shining through the rain clouds appears to be surrounded by a halo, the rain will soon stop, but a halo round the moon shows a long period of rain within three days. Likewise if the crescent moon appears to have her horns tilted upwards, she is holding her water: the weather will be fine. But if the horns are tilted downwards, it will be showery. When the full moon rises large and golden in the sky, a period of warm weather is in store. But if she rises small and bright, cold silver, then the next day will be cold, possibly frosty. The major changes in the weather always seem to occur at the moon's quarters. If it doesn't change then it will usually stay the same for another week.

STARS   If the stars are small and seem to blink, there will be wind the next day. If they are large and blink, there will be wind and rain, but if the stars are large, clear and steady, fresh fine weather is on the way. A thunderstorm at night after a muggy day will leave the air fresh for twelve hours, but lightning at night without the accompaniment of thunder will be followed by a heavy, humid day.

MIST AND FIRES   When you wake up to find a light low mist, you can be sure of a fine day, but if the mist is high over the hills, rain is on the way. A heavy mist that is blown by the wind also presages rain. If the smoke from the fire draws high and straight up into the sky, the weather will be fine, but if the smoke clings to the ground, rain is forecast. When the fire burns bright and steady in the spring or autumn, expect frost next day.

PLANTS   The plants also show us when change is coming. Many flowers close up their petals before rain, most notably the lovely little scarlet pimpernel. When the trees talk to each other expectantly, rustling their leaves on a hot still day, when there is no breeze, you can expect a cloudburst.

CREATURES AND THE WEATHER   If birds become quiet and everything seems to be holding its breath, a thunderstorm is on the way; likewise, when dogs jump about rearranging their bedding, lightning and thunder is in the air. A horse standing with its back to the hedge foretells stormy weather, both wet and windy. Frogs and toads will come out of hiding croaking noisily just before a prolonged period of fine weather comes to an end. Be warned when birds become bolder, scavenging for titbits close to your home in the autumn: you can expect the first wintry weather within three days.

Spiders will repair old webs if bad weather is on the way, but will happily make new ones if the day is to be fine. Ants will build little walls around their nests when it is going to rain. A spiral column of gnats in the evening shows that the next day will be fine, but if flies are 'sticky', annoying people and animals, sluggishly refusing to be brushed away, a storm is brewing.

OTHER ROMANY WEATHER OMENS   Most of the Romanies have their own favourite weather omens. My uncle was a great fund of natural weather lore, but he also used more scientific means of prediction. Whenever we pulled into a place such as an orchard where we knew we would be stopping for several weeks, he would put a narrow necked bottle upside down into a jam jar half filled with water. After being given about twenty-four hours to 'settle down', it would act as a rough, but reliable barometer. The water would rise up the neck of the bottle when rain was on the way, and fall when it was going to be fine.

My uncle was also famed for his ability to tell the time by the sun, even on a cloudy day. He would take off his trilby hat and use it to shade his eyes. Holding his finger up to the sun he would make a great play for measuring the shadows. People would be amazed to find that he was accurate to the minute. It wasn't until many years later that I discovered his secret: he used to keep his watch pinned inside his hat for safety whilst he was working.

CHAPTER TEN

Palmistry and Using a Crystal Ball

Palmistry

Prehistoric man left his palm prints emblazoned on rock faces all over the world. It was one of the earliest forms of art. Although theories abound as to the purpose behind this decoration, unless someone invents a time machine, we will never know for sure why early man loved to leave his signature in this way. One thing is sure; our sensitive ancestors would have been aware of the energy tingling in their palms, and they would have noticed the individual differences in the pattern of lines etched upon them. Perhaps the curious among them would study these lines and ponder their meaning.

Certainly palmistry is mentioned in the ancient historical records of many Eastern cultures and it is probable that the Gypsies were responsible for the spread of palmistry throughout the world. Palmistry is particularly popular with the Romany people because it doesn't need any props or equipment of any kind, an important consideration to nomadic people who need to travel light. Also, palmistry can be practised discreetly, any time, anywhere, as opportunity presents itself. Although every Gypsy psychic will have her own favourite form of divination – Tarot, runes, crystal – almost without exception the art of palmistry would have been the first thing she learned at her mother's knee.

Since the nineteenth century palmistry has been raised almost to the level of a science, deserving of a whole book to itself. Indeed many books have been written on the subject, some by authors who have made a microscopic study of the hand. Although generally tending to agree on the meaning of the major lines, these authorities sometimes have differing opinions as to the meaning of the minor lines, as well as the shapes of the fingers and nails.

The hands can be looked upon as a basic map of our life. Romanies say that the left hand is what we're born with, and the right is what we make of it. If you study your own palm from time to time you will notice that the lines on your right hand do change as time goes on.

There are important chakras in the palms, whose function is connected with both drawing in and emitting energy to and from the other chakras. For instance, healing energy is concentrated in and emitted through the palm. This is one of the reasons why it is so nice to hold hands with someone you love, why a caress brings comfort or soothes pain, why it is good to stroke a pet, touch a tree, hold a crystal ball or trail your hand in running water.

These palm chakras also have to do with our destiny, and the very act of touching someone's hand forges a link that enables the sensitive to tune into the fate of the other person. Thus a Romany reading a palm is essentially reading the chakras, using the lines for guidance. So the lines may show a long journey or change of residence at a certain time, while the chakra will inspire the psychic with more detailed information about the journey, or why the move will take place. A break in a line may show an accident or illness, the chakra will tell what kind of illness or accident is likely.

A Guide to the Palm

Regrettably it is outside the scope of this book to go into the intricate details of such a complex subject as palmistry. Those

interested in making a deeper study of palmistry will find a feast
of books to choose from. But just to start you off, here follows a
basic guide to the palm (see also the diagram on pages 109).

The Lines on the Hand

THE LIFE LINE Among Romany readers, it is generally accepted
that the life line should be roughly divided into ten parts, with each
tenth of the line representing ten years of life. Thus a long life line

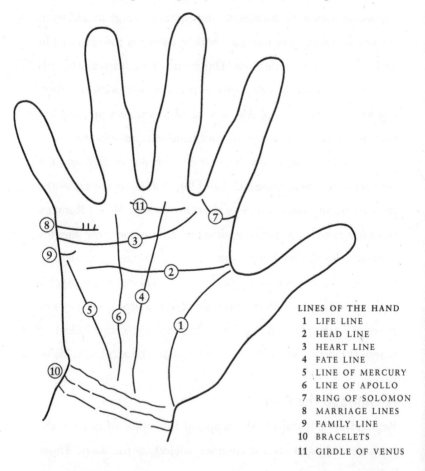

LINES OF THE HAND
1 LIFE LINE
2 HEAD LINE
3 HEART LINE
4 FATE LINE
5 LINE OF MERCURY
6 LINE OF APOLLO
7 RING OF SOLOMON
8 MARRIAGE LINES
9 FAMILY LINE
10 BRACELETS
11 GIRDLE OF VENUS

curling round to the wrist indicates an exceptionally long life. However a short life line does not necessarily mean a short life – other factors must be taken into consideration. The colour and depth of the line is important. A good strong-looking line indicates good health and a confident character, while a faint line could indicate a weak constitution. Chains and breaks in the line indicate illness and accidents, while branches show long journeys or a change of lifestyle.

THE HEAD LINE   The average head line reaches a little over three-quarters of the way across the palm. A longer line can indicate either a great intelligence or a person who is a thinker rather than a doer. Again, as with all the lines, colour and depth should be considered. A deep, unmarked head line can denote an untroubled life, whilst a chained line shows problems to be overcome. Tiny lines fringing the head line indicate wide-ranging interests. When this line gently slopes downwards it shows imagination, but a steep downwards curve can indicate a person who is overimaginative and impractical. A line that goes straight across the palm denotes a practical, single-minded person. A line branching upwards from the head line, towards the heart line, indicates a reliance on other people. This is a person who needs to be told what to do; he will cheerfully allow a partner, employer or religious group to take over his life. A head line that curves upwards towards the fingers is a sign of an exceptionally selfish person, someone who is sure of their own superiority.

THE HEART LINE   A strongly marked heart line is the sign of a warm, faithful, loving character. When the line is smooth and unmarked, the person will be untroubled by the uncertainties and pitfalls that usually accompany the search for love. Either they will marry their first love, or be serenely indifferent to romance. A chained heart line can indicate a flirt, while tiny lines crossing the heart line denote many light relationships. A break in the line indicates a break in a relationship. This does not always mean a lover's quarrel; it may indicate a family dispute or the ending of a friendship.

THE FATE LINE   This is sometimes thought of as the line of success. If the fate line is deep in colour and unbroken, the person has all the attributes to become successful. If the fate line ends at the head line, the subject may not have the will power to overcome obstacles. Alternatively, he may not have the education to fulfil his ambitions. If the line ends at the heart line, emotional ties or duty may get in the way. A broken or chained line shows life will not be easy, and there will be many setbacks to overcome. A line that continues strongly up to the fingers promises true success. Sometimes the line may be pale or broken from the wrist to the head line, but become strong above it; this is often seen when success comes late in life, such as when a woman who has put her family first until her children are grown starts a new career. Of course not everyone's idea of success is the same. To one person it can mean riches and fame, to another a quiet life in the country.

THE LINE OF MERCURY   Named after the messenger of the Roman gods, this line shows a love of study and intellectual pursuits. It is often found on the hands of writers or people involved in communication. It is also found on the hand of dowsers, healers and other psychics.

THE LINE OF APOLLO   Denoting talent and creativity, characteristics of the Roman god of the sun, a long, well-marked Apollo line indicates the person will be able to make their fortune through their own ability.

THE RING OF SOLOMON   Named for the wise King Solomon, this is a sign of an old soul, and denotes wisdom and occult ability.

MARRIAGE LINES   There can be several of these lines in a subject's hand, each one denoting a marriage or close relationship. Small lines going upwards from the marriage line show the number of children. Some Romanies say that deep lines represent boys, faint lines girls.

FAMILY LINE   When this line is deeply marked the person will belong to a close-knit family. It is probable that family ties will have a great influence on his life.

THE BRACELETS   Romanies say that wealth and luck are denoted by three well-defined bracelets. The deeper and clearer the lines, the more fortunate the person will be. Two bracelets are normal, while if there is only one, or if the bracelets are faint or chained, there will be difficulties to overcome. The bracelets are also an indication of health and well-being.

THE GIRDLE OF VENUS   Named for the Roman goddess of love, this line shows a sensual, well-developed sex drive. The longer and deeper this line, the more developed the sexual nature. A person with this line is usually attractive to the opposite sex.

TRAVEL LINES   Short lines and forks denote movement and travel. A long, well-developed line indicates the person may live and work abroad.

The following marks have influence over whichever area of the palm on which they appear:

Arrow	Unexpected events
Circle	Danger
Cross	Frustration
Hatching	Delay
Oval	Talent and persistence brings rewards
Square	Difficulties, but they will be overcome
Star	Success
Triangle	Good luck
Trident, fork	Protection, security

The Mounts of the Hand

THE MOUNT OF VENUS   A normal mount of Venus indicates a warm and affectionate nature, and when especially fleshy it shows an overly sensual nature. This person may find it hard to establish a loving relationship, seeking only sexual gratification.

THE MOUNT OF THE MOON   This mount is connected with intuition and imagination, and is often well developed in the hands of artists and psychics, although an overdeveloped mount can indicate a person who lives too much in his or her own imagination. Conversely

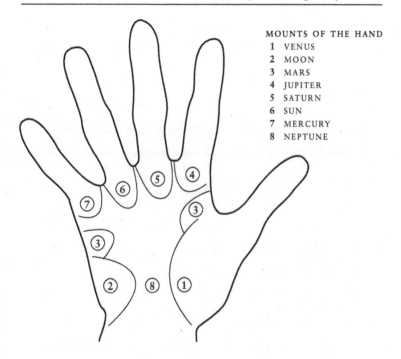

MOUNTS OF THE HAND
1 VENUS
2 MOON
3 MARS
4 JUPITER
5 SATURN
6 SUN
7 MERCURY
8 NEPTUNE

an underdeveloped mount can also indicate an unbalanced outlook on life. The mount of the moon is also an indication of the warmth of the personality, and the way in which the person relates to others. A normal mount indicates a well-balanced, friendly outlook. When the mount is overdeveloped, it denotes a weak, sentimental mind, while an underdeveloped mount often indicates a born troublemaker, one who enjoys the misfortune of others.

THE MOUNT OF MARS The size of this mount (named for the Roman god of war) reveals a person's courage, determination and aggressive tendencies. A normal mount indicates a person who will stand his ground; though not aggressive, he will not back away from confrontation. A large mount often denotes a fiery, aggressive nature, whilst a small mount will be found on the hand of a weak, perhaps cowardly person.

THE MOUNT OF JUPITER   Named for the jolly king of the Roman gods, when the mount is normally developed the person will be comfortably off. He or she may be ambitious but not overly so, and their outlook on life is usually cheerful and optimistic. An underdeveloped mount can show a lack of these qualities, whilst an overdeveloped mount indicates a proud nature. This person will be driven by ambition. An overdeveloped mount of Jupiter can be found on the palm of dictators and megalomaniacs.

THE MOUNT OF SATURN   Life is a learning process, full of difficulties to be overcome. Named for the old man of the Roman gods, the mount of Saturn can indicate the way in which each of us will face up to those challenges. A normal mount shows a trustworthy person who will try to overcome life's obstacles with dignity. An overdeveloped mount indicates that the person will be confronted with many problems, and a large mount can sometimes be found on the hand of a bitter or morbid person. A small mount denotes an unhappy life.

THE MOUNT OF THE SUN   A normal mount denotes an optimistic and sunny personality. This person will usually be courteous, showing dignity and good taste in all things. A large mount belongs to a boastful, larger-than-life character, whilst a small mount can indicate a mean, cynical nature.

THE MOUNT OF MERCURY   This mount, named after the messenger of the Roman gods, has a bearing on the intelligence of the subject as well as his or her ability to communicate. A large mount shows a person with an overdeveloped opinion of his own intellect – a know-all, probably fond of his own voice. A well-shaped, normal mount denotes an intelligent, articulate person, while an underdeveloped mount shows a lack of education, the inability to concentrate and a certain laziness.

THE MOUNT OF NEPTUNE   Named for the Roman god of the sea, a life of travel is indicated when this mount is present. It also denotes a love of water.

Knowledge of the lines and other features of the hand is of course an essential part of palmistry for the Gypsy reader; a very credible and accurate picture is obtained using the lines alone. However, as the practitioner gains experience and learns to become sensitive to the chakra energy flowing from the client's palm he will be aware that he can divine more about that person's future than the lines alone can tell him.

There is also a down side to opening yourself up in such a direct way to the other person's energy. As you are actually touching the other person, rather than using the cards, crystal or some other tool as an intermediary, there is a danger of absorbing negative energy from the client, especially as many people who request a reading are sad or confused. For this reason I would not attempt to read a palm when depressed or under the weather myself. At such times it can be difficult to shield oneself from the client's unhappiness, which – when added to one's own troubles – can become an intolerable burden.

How to Read Palms

To read the future, take hold of the client's right hand and compose yourself as described earlier. Study the shape of the hand, the major lines and the mounts, then scrutinise the major lines and the relationship of the different features to each other. For a longer reading that includes the past, and for a really detailed character reading, study both hands, taking special note of the differences between the left and the right palms. As already mentioned, the left palm describes that which is given us at birth, such as our basic character and the general outline of our fortune. The right hand shows the future we make for ourselves.

Once you have gained confidence in your ability to correctly interpret the lines, you will find the patterns of the hand will inspire a story or even a vision that will surprise the client with its accuracy. Now you have started to tune into the chakras, you can really read the palm!

The Crystal Ball

The image of the Gypsy, coin-fringed scarf tied over her hair, huddled portentously over her crystal ball, is a very familiar one, popularised through film, novel and frequently newspaper cartoon. Most people, when entering a fortune-teller's booth, would be disappointed not to see a crystal ball prominently displayed on the table. Even though it is the preferred fairground method, the crystal is the one that relies the most on the psychic ability of the seer. Palmistry and Tarot provide signs and symbols to help tell the future, so the crystal is the method most likely to be faked.

I do not mean that every fairground fortune-teller is a fake; on the contrary, some are exceptionally talented psychics. It is just that no one, no matter how talented, is psychic all of the time. It is not something that can be turned on and off like a tap. Doing several readings one after the other can be exhausting mentally and physically, and reading for a constant stream of clients, day in, day out, is impossible. But, given the right conditions, the crystal can provide the most accurate and detailed reading.

The crystal ball is one of several things that come under the larger heading of scrying, which means gazing into an object in order to see visions. This has been done since the dawn of time and many things have been utilised for this purpose: natural pools, polished mirrors, bowls or glasses of clear water, polished stones, bowls of black ink, to name just a few. It is also possible to see visions by looking through the hole in a hag stone. The Gypsies used to say that one could see visions of fairyland in this way.

Although the clear crystal ball is the one most commonly seen, other colours have been used with great effect. Balls of rose quartz or amethyst were once popular, and I know of someone who loves to use a ball of black glass. A ball is by definition round, of course, but ovoid 'balls' were once very well liked too, and if one prefers to hold the ball rather than have it on a stand the egg shape fits comfortably into the palms.

Nowadays one would have to be almost a millionaire to be able to afford a ball made from rock crystal, and even a good lead crystal glass ball is expensive. Luckily a nice clear glass ball is quite acceptable, or even a bowl of water as mentioned above. Although rock crystal is a sensitive, living substance and a wonderful tool, as it is especially good at picking up the subtle vibrations in the zee energy, any shiny surface can be used to concentrate on.

When buying your crystal ball, look for one that feels good to you. The size, shape, colour, or any imperfections are immaterial as long as it feels right to the person who is using it.

Wash your crystal in clear water to which a little salt and a drop of perfumed oil have been added. Amber or sandalwood are ideal. This will cleanse it of any unwelcome influences that it may have accrued in the past. Dry it on a new cloth. You may like to light a candle and some incense, and say a little prayer to welcome the crystal into your life.

Keep your crystal covered with a black or purple cloth. This is not just to keep the ball safe from negative influences, but is also a safety precaution. The crystal magnifies the sun's rays, and can easily start a fire. Not long ago my husband happened to be holding a crystal ball outdoors on a cloudy spring day. In a few moments his jumper was smouldering where the sun's rays, weak though they were, had shone through the crystal. So be warned!

Keep your crystal for at least a week before attempting to use it. Hold it frequently, passing your hands over its surface. It is a good idea to polish it sometimes with a scrap of black silk, which should be kept for the purpose.

Crystal-gazing

Attempt your first crystal-gazing when the phase of the moon is
dark or just new. Choose a time when things are quiet and you are
unlikely to be disturbed. The light should be steady, not shining
directly on to the crystal or into your eyes. A good time of day for
this is in the evening when the sun has set, but before dark. This is
a magical time, a transition from one time to the next, but if this is
impossible arrange the lighting appropriately. Burn some amber or
sandalwood perfume. Sit comfortably before your crystal ball.
There are no fixed rules as to how you should sit, or how far away
the ball should be, just as long as it feels right.

Take the cover off the crystal and quieten your mind (page
20). Pass your hands three times around the ball, almost but not
quite touching it. Feel the energy jumping between the ball and
your palms, then relax. Look into the ball steadily, but not
fixedly; nothing should feel difficult or forced. Your eyes will
probably slip out of focus. This is natural; let it happen. Don't
try too long – half an hour is long enough for the first attempt.

It is unlikely that you will see anything in the crystal the first
time you try to use it, or even the first few times. It takes practice,
but persistence will pay off eventually. The first sign is usually a
clouding of the crystal; sometimes these clouds are white,
sometimes coloured. The clouds will gradually clear and visions
will start to appear. The first time this happens the surprise will
usually bring the seer back to earth with a bump, banishing the
visions for the time being. But being better prepared for this
development, the next session should be more successful.

Different people see the crystal visions in different ways. Some see the visions actually in the crystal as tiny pictures, while for others the crystal vanishes and the visions appear in front of their eyes. Some see symbols that they have to interpret, whilst others see actual events. It is a good idea to approach the crystal with a question in mind, or a place or person you would like to see, otherwise the visions are likely to be a meaningless mish-mash.

When reading for another person, the same steps should be followed, but that person should be the one to pass their hands over the ball. Ask them to clear their minds and concentrate on what it is they wish to know. Don't attempt to use the crystal for anyone else until you are confident in your ability, or nervousness will lead to failure.

Once you are proficient you will be able to use the crystal anywhere, anytime. You will be able to shut out the distractions of the outside world, and pass into the world of visions at will. But don't expect this to happen overnight. As I said earlier, crystal-grazing or scrying in any form are methods of seeing the future that rely purely on the psychic powers of the seer, without help from cards, palms, or any other aids to prediction. It is the art that requires the most dedication, practice and perseverance if the seer is to fulfil their true potential through it.

Working with the Tarot

As a very young child, I was lucky enough to be given a Tarot pack to play with. There must have been several cards missing or they would not have been discarded in this way, but I spent many happy hours arranging and rearranging them, making up stories about the different characters depicted upon them. Later, I was allowed to sit with my grandmother while she read the 'Wardi' (Tarot) cards for her clients. Watching and learning, I would silently make up my own stories from the way the cards were dealt, and would be pleased to find how similar my stories were to hers.

When I grew a little older and started school, I would sometimes take my cards with me to play at fortune-telling for my friends, until one day I was caught in the act by Sister Clare Veronica, one of the teaching nuns. She angrily confiscated my cards calling them 'an abomination of the Devil' and me a 'child of Satan'. I didn't know what that meant at the time, but I knew it was something bad when I was soundly caned in front of the whole class.

I never saw my beloved Tarot pack again, but nothing could spoil my fascination with the cards. It's a fascination that has lasted to this day. The Tarot is still my favourite method of 'dukering' – that is, fortune telling.

The beginnings of the Tarot are veiled in mystery. There are theories as to the cards' origins; the occasional historical reference exists from the Middle Ages, but there is little concrete information. I have been told that paintings found on the walls of an ancient Egyptian temple dedicated to Thoth, the god of wisdom, have the same symbolic meaning as the cards of the major arcana, but to date I have found no confirmation of this.

The Tarot seems to strike a cord in the psyche as the epitome of mystery. Many people who are quite happy to have their palm read tremble at the thought of having a Tarot reading, though I find it to be probably the most helpful and sympathetic type of reading of all. The Tarot seems to get to the heart of the client's most pressing problems, giving advice or hope for the future.

There are shelves full of books on the Tarot, and each writer will have his or her own 'slant' on interpreting the cards. Of course the Tarot is much more than a system of fortune telling; it is a method of teaching arcane truth. You will find that some books concentrate on that aspect of the cards, the inner spiritual journey of initiation, and although this is arguably the most important function of the cards it is of little use to an enquirer troubled by the everyday business of living. So I will share with you the more mundane meaning of the cards favoured by the Romanies when reading for a client.

Working With Tarot Cards

The first step is to find the right cards. This can be a quest in itself. Nowadays there are dozens of packs to choose from, from the *Mythical Tarot* to the *Tarot of Witches*, from the *Norse Tarot* to those based on the Native American cultures, as well as the classical decks. You will find a Tarot for every path and inclination. So take your time, and have a good look at all the available decks before choosing.

Look for a pack that resonates with your psyche, one that you are truly drawn to, not one that you think you should like. For instance, don't automatically choose the *Witches Tarot* if you are a follower of Wicca, or the Norse pack if you are interested in the Rune lore, unless you find the images truly powerful. Some of the more recent packs strike me as a being little too pretty or twee, but this is purely a personal view. These particular images may be exactly what's needed by a complete beginner who may be a little overawed by the stronger images of some older packs. Most Gypsy readers use the Marseilles Tarot or, more often, my own favourite: the Rider Waite Tarot.

The Tarot is divided into two parts, the major arcana and the minor arcana. The major arcana consists of twenty-two deeply symbolic picture cards; these can be taken to represent man's journey through life, or the seeker's journey into initiation. The minor arcana has four suits, which are wands, swords, cups and pentacles, which roughly correspond with those of normal playing cards, that is, clubs, spades, hearts and diamonds. Each of the Tarot suits consists of four court cards and ten numbered cards. In some packs the numbered cards are only given pips – for instance, four swords or four wands – whilst in other packs all the cards have meaningful pictures. This is another consideration to take into account when choosing your Tarot. I prefer a pack that has pictures rather than pips, as I find this much more inspiring, and if you are a beginner it saves the worry of having to remember a list of meanings without having anything to prompt your memory.

Starting to Work With Your Own Cards

When you have purchased your Tarot pack, make or buy a cloth in which to wrap it. Black silk is a good choice, or maybe dark blue or violet. The cloth should be large enough for cards to be laid out on it when you are doing a reading, but not so large as to be bulky. Some people like to keep everything in a special box.

Light a blue or violet candle and some sandalwood, frankincense or amber incense. Welcome the cards into your life with a prayer of thanks. You should take the cards out of the box and shuffle them well over and over again, as the Gypsies say this puts the life or the zee energy into the cards. Become used to handling them. For the first week or so, keep the cards near to you in a handbag or pocket. Look at them or just touch

Every Tarot pack comes with its own little instruction booklet, which will give a basic grounding as to the meaning of the cards. Study each card in turn whenever the opportunity arises. Notice the colours, each detail of the design; every tiny element has been included for a purpose. Be sure that you are completely familiar with your cards before attempting a reading. By this I don't mean that you should be word perfect as to the accepted meanings of the cards, but you should be familiar with the look and feel of them. You should be confident that your cards are alive with zee energy, and that you have made them yours.

them whenever possible. This will help to tune the cards into your own personal energy.

Once you are confident in handling your cards, try a reading for yourself, or for a close friend whom you can trust not to laugh at your first efforts. A useful spread to start with is the simple nine-card Gypsy oracle. The cards are dealt in three rows of three. The top row is the past, the centre the present, the bottom row is what is to come. This spread gives good practice in reading the cards together as a story, without it being too long or complicated.

No card is good or bad in itself. Each should be read in context, together with those besides it, and its place in the spread. You should also take note of the 'feel' you get from the card. I have known a card to feel really evil in one reading, but quite pleasant in the next. Note what part of the design immediately catches your eye. Is it some symbol in the background, or the figure in the foreground? What is the overall colour of the reading? Is it bright and hopeful, or dark and gloomy? Is there a predominance of one suit? For instance, the presence of lots of cups could mean that the client's emotional life takes centre stage for a while, whereas a predominance of pentacles may show property, work or money matters will be dominating for a while. Particular note should be taken when cards of the major arcana appear in the spread. Any influence shown by the presence of one of these cards is of special importance. Now and again you will find a card is reversed, dealt upside down. This usually puts a negative meaning on the card.

For example, the Six of Pentacles reversed could mean the client spending money not receiving it, or the Ace of Wands reversed could signify a new project aborted.

Begin your reading by shuffling the pack to reinvigorate the zee energy, then if you are reading for someone else ask him or her to shuffle the cards. The client should then cut the cards into three using their left hand, then put them all together again into one pile. Deal the cards face upwards on to the cloth in which you keep them. Take a moment to compose yourself for the reading as instructed in earlier pages.

Examine all the cards before you begin in order to get the feel of the reading. There is no need to rush. Once you start you will find that the story will come to you almost of its own volition. Don't worry if you have forgotten the accepted meaning of a certain card; just say what it means to you in the context of the reading.

I like to start with the present and the client's state of mind, then go back to the past, the influences that have brought about the current situation, then on to the future outcome. There is no clear-cut line between the three times. The past can include the present, and the present can include the near future.

There are occasions when parts of a reading seem to make no sense. Don't be afraid to explain this to the client. It could be that at the time of the reading the client's life is a complete confusion of emotions or events, or it may be better for the client's karma if that person works out that particular period for him- or herself. Of course, some people are just terribly difficult to read for. It may be something to do with their emotional state, or that their mind is on anything but the reading. For such people reading can be like trying to run through treacle. Explain that you are finding it difficult. Sometimes they will admit that other psychics have had the same problem. You just have to soldier on and do your best.

Always shuffle the cards again at the end of a reading and wrap the pack in its special cloth. This wipes the cards clean of any lingering influences that may be left by the previous client. The act of wrapping the cards helps to bring you back into the normal world. It is also a signal to the occasional persistent client that there is nothing more to be told; the reading is definitely over.

When to Consult the Cards

One thing I am often asked is, 'Is it unlucky to read the cards for oneself?' On the contrary, when used correctly the Tarot can be an exceedingly helpful friend. But – human nature being what it is – there can be pitfalls. Firstly, it is difficult to read the Tarot for oneself. When reading for strangers, unless they have asked a specific question there are no preconceptions. One's psyche is free to interpret the cards without bias. When reading for oneself, however, the interpretation is coloured by all the things that are going on in one's life, with all the attendant hopes and fears, so there is no chance of an unbiased reading.

Which leads me to the second problem. If one doesn't like a reading there is a tendency to repeat it until one gets a reading that is more promising. Conversely, if the reading promises luck and happiness it may sound too good to be true, so there is a temptation to do it again just to make sure. Either way, if a reading is repeated several times, you will just end up with nonsense.

Thirdly, it is too easy to become over-reliant on the Tarot by consulting it for every little problem, or becoming unable to take the smallest step without asking the cards for help. This is clearly unwise and unhealthy.

I find it best to consult the Tarot about the future only when I am very worried or depressed, or when there is an important decision about which I find it impossible to make up my mind. Even then I try to limit myself to a three-card answer.

The Basic Meaning of the Tarot Cards

The Major Arcana

THE FOOL   The Fool is the only card of the major arcana that is not numbered. The Fool can be the beginning or the end. On one level it represents the newborn child ready to start his journey through life; on another it is the novice setting out on his quest for initiation. Innocence, enthusiasm, awe, wonder, bravery, optimism, self-confidence: all are represented by the Fool. It is a card of new beginnings and new hope, and signifies throwing caution to the wind, enjoying the journey. It also represents the goal of initiation, and on a mundane level the state of mind we should hope to achieve at the end of life's journey. Only when surrounded by cards of caution such as the Ten of Swords does the Fool show rashness and stupidity.

1. THE MAGICIAN   This is a card of ability. It shows that the querent has all the qualifications he needs to make the most of any given situation. When the Magician appears it is time for the querent to show that he has the knowledge and talent for the task in hand and should forget false modesty and take centre stage. This card can also represent a person with these qualities who has influence over the querent's life. A sometimes tricky character, he is someone to have on your side rather than against you. He should not be taken at face value.

2. THE HIGH PRIESTESS   A card of initiation, this is a card of hidden meanings, secrets not ready to be revealed. The High Priestess can show a need to nourish your spiritual nature, to get away from the rat race, or she could just be telling you to follow your hunches. It can also represent a rather otherworldly but a gentle and honest woman.

3. THE EMPRESS   This is a card of growth, security and fulfilment, especially for women or matters pertaining to women. Things come to fruition, or to a satisfactory conclusion. The Empress can also foretell a pregnancy or birth. Sometimes this card can represent a woman who may be a little smug but is always kindly and generous.

4. THE EMPEROR   He denotes a time of opportunity and the chance to better oneself. The querent may find himself in a position of power, or able to advise someone else. Be sure to exercise good sense and fairness. The Emperor may also represent a person such as an employer or father figure – a man sure of his own position, confident and intelligent, or overbearing and pompous.

5. THE HIEROPHANT   This card is in some ways similar in meaning to the High Priestess, except that the Hierophant is more inclined to follow the orthodox view than that imaginative, intuitive lady. This card shows a need to study and love of learning, and can represent a person in a position of authority or a professional man able to advise the querent, someone kindly and well meaning – but remember that there is an iron fist in the velvet glove; the person could be self-righteous and sanctimonious.

6. THE LOVERS   This is not just about love but a card of choices of all kinds, usually between the old and familiar, or the new and exciting, the sensible or the glamorous. To choose one option means the loss of the other, so careful thought is called for.

7. THE CHARIOT   The querent is able to steer his life in whatever direction he wishes when this card appears, but he may find a conflict of interest, or conflicting emotions may leave him undecided as to what course to take. He must be level-headed and positive in order to make progress.

8. STRENGTH   Although physical strength can be indicated by this card, it usually represents strength of will as well as the ability to overcome illness, pain and emotional trauma.

9. THE HERMIT   Several meanings can be drawn from this card. The querent may be looking for something to give his life meaning, such as a religion, a philosophy, or maybe just a new hobby. It may

show that he is too solitary and needs to broaden his horizons. For a businessman or someone looking for work, the Hermit can show the need to find new ideas, or look further afield.

10. THE WHEEL OF FORTUNE   The Wheel turns bringing change, or the opportunity for change. The Wheel always appears at a crossroads in life. Either change is forced on the querent, or he is given a chance to make a difference for himself. Will he take it, or let it slip through his fingers? It's up to him.

11. JUSTICE   You will reap what you sow. In other words you will get what you deserve. If you have done well it will be recognised, if you have done ill – beware, you will be found out. Justice can indicate a need to think clearly, to consider all the facts, to be fair and just to others. There are times when this card predicts actual legal proceedings or an interview when the querent is being judged in some way.

12. THE HANGED MAN   This is a powerfully spiritual card, the meaning of which is self-sacrifice for the greater good. It can also denote putting one's own hopes to one side for the sake of another, doing without now in order to gain in the future. This card can bring spiritual advancement, or on the negative side turn you into a drudge. It is also a card of study, of working to gain knowledge.

13. DEATH   This relates to an ending, perhaps one that brings pain, regret or apprehension. It is always hard to cut the ties with the past, no matter how inevitable or longed for the change may be. Something familiar goes out of your life, but its departure leaves room for new experience.

14. TEMPERANCE This card relates to a time in which the querent should take care and be cautious, keeping a watchful eye on money, health and temper. Extravagance should be avoided, and be careful when exercising. Think before you speak; you may feel like giving someone a piece of your mind, but now is not the time. It may be hard, but you will be thankful later.

15. THE DEVIL Man's baser side is represented by this card: the mundane part that loves comfort and material things. It can represent everything and anything from the innocent desire for a new pair of shoes or a new washing machine to overindulgence in drink, sex and drugs. There is a definite wish to let one's hair down.

16. THE TOWER This relates to a sudden bolt from the blue, an unexpected blow, a change that is hard to come to terms with. It can symbolise an emotional shock, or an accident or damage to a person or property. But the Tower is always built on strong foundations and can be rebuilt. Thus the querent will be able to rebuild his life whatever damage has been inflicted, and become a stronger person for it.

17. THE STAR Bringing luck and hope, the Star predicts improvement in all areas of life. Though the results may not be immediately noticeable, the groundwork is being laid for future happiness.

18. THE MOON Mysterious and ever changing, the Moon can be read in several ways. It may relate to secrets and mystery, to occult power. With it may come a sense that all is not well, or perhaps a longing for what one can never have. It is a card of dreams, ambition and fame, and also of dishonesty, infamy and madness.

19. THE SUN The Sun brings happiness, joy and contentment. Its warm radiance shines on all areas of life. It may relate to a positive time when anything seems possible. On another level the Sun can foretell marriage, pregnancy or birth.

20. JUDGEMENT Judgement marks a new beginning, a new life – the chance to start again, leaving behind past mistakes. Just when all seems dark and depressing, there is hope for the future. Think deeply about what went wrong in the past, and how to take the greatest advantage of this new opportunity.

21. THE WORLD Be it on an emotional, spiritual or material level, the presence of the World suggests that all that has been hoped for is achieved. Great contentment and satisfaction are shown by this card. The querent will have all he needs to make his own particular world complete.

The Cards of the Minor Arcana

CUPS

ACE OF CUPS This is a wonderful card for all matters concerning the heart and emotions: a new love, or a deep and abiding friendship;

alternatively, a closer understanding in an existing relationship. It also
represents spiritual fulfilment and learning.

TWO OF CUPS This signifies a marriage, engagement or similar
emotional commitment, or a business contract or partnership in which
both sides are in total harmony.

THREE OF CUPS This denotes a celebration such as a wedding,
birth or just a party. It can also indicate success in business or exams.

FOUR OF CUPS The querent is in a despondent mood, or maybe just
bored. He is stuck in a rut and finds it hard to take an interest in the
world around him. There is a danger he may miss a great opportunity,
and should try to pull himself out of the mire before it is too late.

FIVE OF CUPS Now the querent is downright depressed, spending
his time brooding over past disappointments and wrongs. The time has
come to put all that behind him, to forgive and forget. The future
could be wonderful if only he would give it a chance.

SIX OF CUPS People from the past, old friends and family members,
reappear in the querent's life. Alternatively there is a return to old
familiar ground, perhaps a childhood home. This can also represent the
querent's children.

SEVEN OF CUPS Ambition, dreams, choices: the possibilities are
endless. This also signifies imagination, talent and romanticism.

EIGHT OF CUPS A card of movement. A relationship may progress to a deeper, more mature level, or alternatively the people involved may find they have outgrown each other. It can also represent actual movement, such as a child leaving home, a journey or a change of address.

NINE OF CUPS The first of the two cards that the Romanies call 'wish cards', relating to happiness, contentment, a celebration, a boost to the ego. Your hopes will be realised. This card brings the kind of intense burst of joy that occasionally adds zing to life.

TEN OF CUPS The second wish card is similar in meaning to the Nine of Cups, but brings long-term contentment, love, happiness and security.

PAGE OF CUPS A new love affair, a proposal or a new friend. This card is also good for intellectual pursuits, particularly metaphysics, alternative medicine and nature.

KNIGHT OF CUPS Your knight in shining armour is on the way, a person fond of the querent, or one willing to help him. It can also show a longing for love. The Knight of Cups can represent a romantic, possibly artistic man.

QUEEN OF CUPS This is a woman who is loving and kind; she may not be very practical, but is concerned about others. Imaginative and artistic, she could have strong powers of intuition. Alternatively, the card can indicate the need to relax, to do what one wants to do, and to take note of one's inner feelings.

KING OF CUPS   This is a man who is sensitive to the feelings of others. Kindly, with a genuine desire to help, and intelligent but imaginative, he could be a professional man such as a doctor.

WANDS

ACE OF WANDS   This card heralds a new venture, be it a journey, a change of address, a pregnancy, a business venture or a turning point in life. The Ace of Wands foretells growth, hope, strength and optimism.

TWO OF WANDS   A wish for expansion, both figurative and actual, is represented here: wanting to break out of the rut, to expand one's knowledge or business. On a different level, there could be plans for a holiday abroad, or thoughts of someone who is far away.

THREE OF WANDS   Things come together – a chance to put plans into action, and see the benefits. This is a time for working and communication while energy is high, and is also good for buying and selling and for all matters to do with travel.

FOUR OF WANDS   This is a joyful card, be it referring to a family reunion or a holiday, a business venture or a new job. The querent will find warmth and acceptance wherever he goes.

FIVE OF WANDS   Everyday life may be getting on top of the

querent. Petty annoyances and difficulties build up, and he is getting ready to snap. He may bring trouble on himself through temper, intolerance or sheer bloody-mindedness, or it could be that someone in his life is giving him a hard time. The querent should take a deep breath and realise that these things will pass as long as he doesn't inflame the situation.

SIX OF WANDS   This represents success in all its forms: triumph over adversity, promotion, fame, success in sport, gambling or legal matters. Whatever the querent is involved in, the result will be to his benefit.

SEVEN OF WANDS   There are difficulties ahead. The querent will need all his strength and endurance to overcome them, but he is in a good position to win through. Alternatively, the querent is someone who loves a fight. He will take up the cudgel on behalf of any cause that catches his imagination, and he will not give in to pressure if he thinks that he is in the right.

EIGHT OF WANDS   Expect the unexpected. Life is about to get very busy, and nothing will go as planned. There is a surprise around every corner, both good and bad. This is a time to be adventurous; grab that unexpected opportunity before it slips away again.

NINE OF WANDS   Times are hard, and difficulties must be overcome – the querent has to take some hard knocks and learn some hard lessons, but he will discover inner strength and courage. He will become a better, more self-reliant person because of the experience.

TEN OF WANDS   The querent is likely to bring trouble down upon himself or those around him through overconfidence or an overbearing attitude. He should listen to well-meaning advice before taking on extra work or financial commitment. There could be a danger of physical collapse through overexertion. Be careful if doing manual work or sport, and do not ignore health problems.

PAGE OF WANDS   This represents new ideas, possibly involving creative effort. It can also signify an enthusiastic young man.

KNIGHT OF WANDS   News arrives – perhaps exam results, a long-awaited decision, or tickets for a holiday. Whatever it is, the querent can now make concrete plans for the future. This card can also bring news about someone far away. Alternatively the Knight of Wands may represent a man in the prime of life. He may be creative with high ideals, or single-minded and arrogant.

QUEEN OF WANDS   She is a lady of many abilities. Creative and full of ideas, she is also practical and down to earth. Warm and loving to people and animals, she is likely to be fond of her home and garden, and she may be interested in herbalism or other forms of alternative medicine. Spiritually she is more likely to turn to paganism than mainstream religion. Alternatively this card can represent the querent's interest in any of the above subjects, or it may show that he could benefit from some kind of alternative medical treatment.

KING OF WANDS   He is a more mature man but young at heart. He is creative and imaginative, but better at thinking up new schemes than putting them into practice. He is enthusiastic about new interests, but soon gets bored. Thus, although he is loveable and means well, he cannot always be relied upon.

SWORDS

ACE OF SWORDS This card represents a breakthrough, a hard-won victory, the start of a new phase of life or project, which the querent may be dreading but will ultimately prove rewarding. It can also mean the overcoming of illness, perhaps through an operation, the cutting away of dead wood from the querent's life, maybe in the form of a divorce, or the end of a long-term commitment.

TWO OF SWORDS The querent may feel that he is living on a knife-edge. There is tension, worry, and the querent may have to keep his emotions and his tongue in check in order to keep the peace. He may stand between two warring factions, so to speak, and should be careful not to take sides. Whatever happens, he cannot force change at this time but should wait for the influence to pass.

THREE OF SWORDS Unavoidable sorrow and heartbreak: this card will always bring sadness, the degree of which can be determined by reading the cards on either side.

FOUR OF SWORDS This is a time to rest, and maybe be alone. It can also point to a slight illness, or recuperation from a longer one. In some cases this card can show enforced isolation and loneliness.

FIVE OF SWORDS   This represents the end of conflict, a time to put things right. Be it a failing business venture or a family quarrel, the querent should realise that the time has come to end it. Even if he is in the right, it will be in his own best interest to cut his losses or seek reconciliation.

SIX OF SWORDS   Leave your troubles behind and sail off to your own particular paradise. This can indicate a holiday or a change of abode. A period of bad luck comes to an end.

SEVEN OF SWORDS   Usually a sinister card, this may denote a trouble-maker who wishes the querent ill or a jealous person who is trying to make trouble. A warning to take care of your possessions, this is a card of loss, even theft.

EIGHT OF SWORDS   The querent is a prisoner of his own emotions. Alternatively a relationship, business or some other commitment keeps him tied down. It is possible that he welcomes the restriction, either through love of what he is doing or because he is trying to fill a gap in his life. Sometimes this card can show immobility through illness, accident or – in some cases – a prison sentence.

NINE OF SWORDS   This card relates to mental torment, depression, worry and nightmares. All kinds of stress and fear are indicated. The cards on either side should be carefully studied in order to find the cause and give hope for the future.

TEN OF SWORDS   This card may have an alarming design, depicting violence, but it is not as bad as it seems. It does indicate disappointment, worry and false hope, but it also shows that the querent is likely to overreact to the situation, take things too much to heart. Perhaps the querent is too fiery or highly strung. There are many disappointments and endings in life, but only by being philosophical about such things can advantage be taken of the new beginning that follows.

PAGE OF SWORDS   Be careful: this card may show that someone is watching you. That person is likely to be a gossip, a spy, or someone in authority who means no good. Any mistake made at this time will be seized upon. The Page of Swords can also represent a young man, surly, aggressive and strong-willed, or one who wears a uniform.

KNIGHT OF SWORDS   Unexpected news or information about legal matters will be coming the querent's way. This card can indicate a situation that quickly comes to a head, or a swift conclusion. The Knight of Swords can represent a man, impetuous, headstrong, often ruthless.

QUEEN OF SWORDS   This is a troubled woman, sometimes lonely or bitter, who can be overbearing and interfering. It can also denote a strong woman who is able to fight her own battles, as well as sadness, endurance, widowhood. In some spreads this can represent the querent's feelings. It can also show that the querent is their own worst enemy, or alternatively, that they bear a heavy burden.

KING OF SWORDS An authoritative man whose head rules his heart, the King of Swords may relate to someone who is usually just but unyielding and unforgiving when wronged. He lives by a strong moral code, and expects others to do the same. He is a good friend but a harsh enemy.

PENTACLES

ACE OF PENTACLES Security, stability, success: this marks a good time to start any new venture concerning business, property, land or investment. It can mean more money on the horizon, either through a windfall, promotion or increased business.

TWO OF PENTACLES This is not a time to be extravagant. There may be a need to juggle financial commitments. The needs of home life and work may conflict, making it hard to strike a balance between the two. Whatever the problem, it is a temporary one.

THREE OF PENTACLES This is an excellent card for the self-employed, the artist or anyone who works with their hands. Ability is recognised and rewarded, and employment is offered. Those employed by another may be offered promotion or a post that enables them to use their own initiative. Those not in work may be asked to use their special talents in some way, or to help with some project, maybe fundraising or community work.

FOUR OF PENTACLES The querent may be worrying about money, but he will always have enough for his needs. This card does not bring riches, but it does bring security. Whatever is spent will be replaced. There is a danger that the querent may become possessive and covetous of material possessions and miserly with money.

FIVE OF PENTACLES   This card shows a difficult patch that, though it may not last long, will be upsetting. It could concern marriage, finance or property. If buying or selling a house, things will not go smoothly. If travel is involved, delays, cancellations, even accidents can be expected.

SIX OF PENTACLES   A windfall, bonus, insurance pay-out, inheritance, gift or lucky win is indicated. However, in a negative spread the querent may be the one paying out.

SEVEN OF PENTACLES   Achievement and security: the querent may not have all he desires, but his efforts are bearing fruit. For the business person or the self-employed, steady growth is forecast.

EIGHT OF PENTACLES   If the querent is prepared to work hard, he will reap the rewards. This indicates a time to take the initiative, and is particularly good for the self-employed and those working with their hands.

NINE OF PENTACLES   The querent has reached a stage in life where he can enjoy a little comfort and luxury, be a little self-indulgent, refurbish his home, or buy a new car. There is a feeling of self-satisfaction about this card as well as security.

TEN OF PENTACLES This is a lovely card for those wishing
to start a family. For older people there is the joy of a caring family
about them. A card of stability, a happy secure home life, and
goals achieved.

PAGE OF PENTACLES This card may relate to an idea that can be
turned into a money-making scheme, a new job or the first steps
towards moving house. The Page of Pentacles can also represent a
young but sensible man, practical about financial matters and business
affairs. On the negative side, he can be shrewdly calculating and cold-
hearted when money is involved.

KNIGHT OF PENTACLES The Knight can denote news about
financial matters, insurance, business or home affairs. He may be a sign
that something concerning these issues is coming to a head or drawing
to a close. This card shows the need to be sensible and clear-sighted. It
may also indicate an intelligent, hard-working person – someone who
will make their own way in life. Sometimes it shows the influence of a
professional person such as an accountant or a solicitor.

QUEEN OF PENTACLES She relates to a female of similar
character to the Knight of Pentacles. She may seem a little cold and
overly interested in material possessions, but she will never let down
her family or close friends. Alternatively, if the querent is female and
unemployed she may feel the need to earn money for herself rather
than just be a housewife. If the querent is male this card can represent
the feelings of his partner.

KING OF PENTACLES A man who is intelligent, practical, successful, he can succeed in all that he sets out to do. Reliable, generous and a good friend, he will do all that he can to provide for his dependants. This card can sometimes represent a professional person consulted by the querent who will be trustworthy and fair.

Sample Spreads and Readings

There are of course, lots of different spreads or methods of laying out the cards for a reading. Each tarot reader will have his or her own favourite. I have illustrated three spreads that I find can be adapted effectively to suit any reading whether it is a specific question or a general look at the future.

The Nine-Card Gypsy Oracle

This spread is very useful when a short reading is called for (see diagram on page 143). It can be used to provide an overview of the general trends in the client's life, or be focused on a particular problem. The top line of three cards represents the past, the second line reflects the present, and the bottom line predicts the future.

A Sample Reading

The client had just moved house to a rather isolated location and was wondering if he had done the right thing; the decision to move was taken on the spur of the moment.

The first line of cards representing the past includes the Seven

Past:

SEVEN OF
WANDS

THE DEVIL

KNIGHT OF
CUPS

Present:

THE CHARIOT

JUDGEMENT

THE HANGED
MAN

Future:

SIX OF
CUPS

QUEEN OF
WANDS

THE TOWER

of Wands, showing that the querent felt he was in a constant struggle to keep on top of things. Although his true nature, represented by the Knight of Cups, is romantic and imaginative, his circumstances, shown by the Devil, were keeping him tied to the rat race.

The second line of cards, the present, shows him deciding to steer his life along a different road (the Chariot), while Judgement has him achieving his goal of moving from the city to a new life in the country. The Hanged Man indicates that this involves certain sacrifices and hard work, possibly more than expected.

The last line predicts the move will be good for the happiness and well-being of the whole family (Six of Cups and Queen of Wands). Unfortunately the Tower in the final position shows that an outside influence may force them to move again. My feeling was that this would be the result of money problems. However I did feel that all is not lost. The work and improvement put into the property is likely to pay dividends, providing a profit to be invested in another home.

The Three-Card Answer

For this spread the querent is asked to shuffle the cards whilst he concentrates on one particular question. He should then take three cards from anywhere in the pack. The cards should be laid down one at a time and read in the order in which they are drawn. Up to three questions can be effectively answered in a reading.

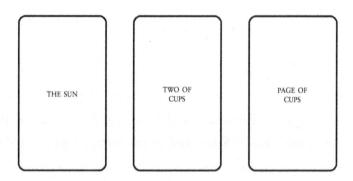

A Sample Reading

This was for a thirty-year-old woman who had been divorced for five years. She swore she would never trust another man, but had recently met someone to whom she was drawn. Although she felt that this man was fond of her, she was holding back her feelings for fear of being hurt.

The Sun is there in the first position, promising joy and happiness through this relationship. Indeed the Two of Cups shows a permanent relationship, possibly marriage, between these two people. The Page of Cups completes this line, showing that although this may be something of a whirlwind romance the feeling on both sides is deep and enduring.

The Celtic Cross

Possibly the most familiar and widely used spread, the Celtic Cross is useful for a more detailed reading. The first card represents the querent: it gives an insight into his personality and indicates his innermost feelings, his mood of the moment. The second card is placed horizontally over the first, forming the

Small Cross: this shows what crosses the querent, in other words indicating the nature of the problem uppermost in his mind. The third card goes above the first two: it shows what crowns him and predicts the best he can achieve in the next month or two. The fourth card goes below the Small Cross, and the fifth card to the right of the Cross. These relate to the past circumstances that have brought about the present situation. Both should be considered together with the cards of the Small Cross in order to gain a deeper understanding of the situation. The sixth is placed to the left of the Small Cross, and relates to the near future.

Four cards are then positioned in a vertical line to the right of the Small Cross. These are dealt from the bottom upwards. The seventh card – being the lowest – indicates what action the querent can take to influence the outcome. The eighth card shows what outside influences will affect his home or work environment in the near future. The ninth card shows the querent's hopes or fears – what he expects will happen. The tenth predicts what will happen, the real outcome of the situation. The third, sixth and tenth cards should be studied together to get a full picture of the future.

The main spread of the cross predicts the next month or two. However I was taught to put two further lines of seven cards each beneath the cross in order to look further into the future. These two rows are dealt from right to left but read from left to right. In certain circumstances, for example if the last row is very unclear or very gloomy, I will deal another round of seven cards. Sometimes this will clarify things or show happier circumstances to look forward to. At other times this third row will just be a

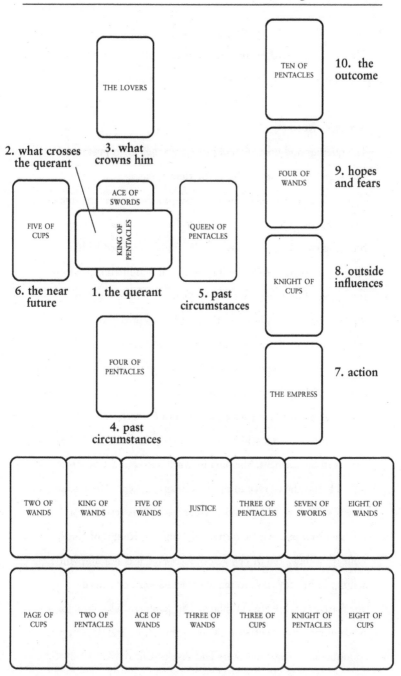

resume of the whole reading, in which case it is best left at that.

This type of reading usually works itself out in six months to a year, the last lines showing two or three months each.

A Sample Reading

The querent and his wife had just set up their own business. He was wondering if he had done the right thing.

The Ace of Swords in the first position shows that the querent has had difficulties in the past but feels he has made a great breakthrough in starting his own business, as indeed he has. The King of Pentacles proves he has the talent and intelligence to be successful, though its position shows he may have niggling doubts about his abilities. In the past he has dreamed about starting his own business, but until now the need for economic security while bringing up a family has stopped him. It is possible that the money and impetus for this new venture has come from his wife (Four of Pentacles and Queen of Pentacles).

The coming week will be an inspirational one. He will find his wife is in her element. She puts forward a new and workable idea. He has the chance to put this before a client. The querent is sure the client will be pleased, which he is. This results in a contract that promises security (the Empress, Knight of Cups, Four of Wands, Ten of Pentacles). However, it is not all plain sailing, as he may have to make choices about, or consider alternatives to, his original plans. This dampens his spirits for a while as he was so enthusiastic about his ideas, and doesn't want to moderate them (the Lovers and Five of Cups).

The next few months bring an expansion of the business (Two of Wands). The good work already done will build up the reputation of the business bringing in new orders (Justice and Three of Pentacles). Difficulties may arise because of the increasing volume of work, which could lead to carelessness bringing about a loss (Seven of Swords). However, the querent finds he enjoys the stimulation and rises to the challenging circumstances (Eight of Wands).

He may need to take on extra staff at this time (Page of Cups), although this may seem like unnecessary expense with the need to juggle finances at this stage in the business (Two of Pentacles). But there are new opportunities for expansion, probably connected to overseas contacts (Ace of Wands, Three of Wands). This is a successful move, and there is every indication that the overseas business will continue to grow (Three of Cups, Knight of Pentacles, Eight of Cups). I have no hesitation in telling this client that he has done the right thing in starting his own business.

Some Simple Spells

A spell can mean several things, from a complicated rite lasting several days, to a simple charm like spitting on a coin found in the street. Even a flirtatious glance across a room can be said to cast a spell in various circumstances. In earlier pages we took a step into spellcraft with the making of the duk rak and duk koor, and also with the making and dedicating of talismans. A Romany choovihni – wise woman – will often create a new spell to suit the occasion. Given the basic knowledge of colour, perfume, herb and symbolism, you can do the same (see Chapter 6 for some correspondences). However, there are many tried and tested spells that have been used with success by generations of Romany people – some very simple, others more complicated. The words would be spoken in Romanes, the Romany language, but I have translated several which are useful in enhancing different areas of life.

A Spell For Attracting Material Goods

This is a deceptively simple but exceedingly effective spell for attracting material goods of any description into your life – be they a car, new furniture, clothes or whatever. Write down whatever it is you desire on a clean sheet of paper or, alternatively, obtain a sketch or photo of the same. Place the paper or photo on a small square of green cloth. Concentrate on it for a few moments. Try to visualise the thing before you, the shape, texture, colour. Feel pride in owning the thing, the pleasure you hope it will bring, what you will do with it.

Then pick up the paper or photo and hold it to your forehead, saying three times, 'I have you, I hold you, I keep you.'

Fold the paper into the green cloth, then tie it round with a length of red thread or wool. Tie seven knots into the wool. As you tie each knot, say, 'You are mine. I own you.' Put the whole in a small box of some kind. Each day, for seven days, hold the box to your forehead and say three times, 'You are mine, I own you.' Put the box away in the back of a drawer.

The above spell can be adapted to bring success in business dealings, job interviews or anything at all to do with the material side of life: just write down what it is you want to achieve. If there is a sum of money you need for a specific purpose, write a cheque to yourself for the exact amount, then follow the steps given above.

Another spell that can be adapted to bring any kind of material success, or indeed any purpose, uses the power of trees to help you achieve your aim.

A Spell Using the Power of Trees

Write down your wish on a clean sheet of paper, then wrap the paper round a coin or some small trinket. Take a parcel, a small bread roll and a little wine, beer or spring water. Find a thorn, elder or ash tree and kneel by the tree and break the roll into crumbs; scatter them round the base of the tree, saying, 'Tree mother, I feed you; feed me in return.' Empty the liquid in the same way, saying, 'Tree mother, I quench your thirst; quench mine in return.' Make a hole near the base of the tree, saying, 'Tree mother, I bring you a gift; bless me in return.' Bury your paper-wrapped coin. Next put both hands on the tree, saying three times, 'Rain falls, wind blows, sun shines, grass grows.' Walk away from the tree without looking back. After three days return to the tree and pick up anything that may be lying on top of the place where you buried your coin. This may be a leaf, twig, feather or small stone. It could even be a ringpull from a can. Carry this thing with you for luck.

Once you have cast one of the above spells, start acting as if it were a foregone conclusion that you will soon be in possession of your heart's desire. If you want a car, buy a mascot for it or some polish. If you want a pony, buy some bits for the harness. Pick up bits and pieces for your new home. Make a detailed plan of how you will spend your money. Soon you will start metaphorically to fall over different versions of your longed-for possession. In the unlikeliest places you will be given books about or pictures of it, read articles about it, find a broken one or parts of an old one. It may be too big, too small, not quite right – but at last your ideal

---

A simpler variation on the above spell is to write down your wish and wrap the paper around a coin or trinket as before, but this time tie it securely with a red thread. Now go to the bank of a river or stream. Holding the coin above your head, turn round nine times, saying, 'Rain falls, wind blows, sun shines, grass grows.' Now throw the parcel into the water as far downstream as you can.

---

will be in your hands. That's how things work.

The Romany people have long known that the glands in the armpit can emit a strongly attractive force that today we call pheromones. It is an old Gypsy trick to tame a horse or dog by feeding them a little bit of bread or cheese that has been kept in the armpit for a while. The animal will become inseparable from its master.

A person going to a job interview or in any situation where it is important to make a good impression and be remembered will increase their chance of success if, before going into the meeting, they hold their right hand under the left armpit and say, 'I am here, see only me; I am here, hear only me. I draw you, I hold you, I draw you, I hold you, I draw you to my will.'

When you shake hands with someone after keeping it under your armpit – and, no, it doesn't have to be a smelly armpit – you will transfer your pheromones and attract them to you. They will think of you constantly without knowing why.

If you are starting a new business or other important venture, you will need all the magical help you can get to ensure success. In the previous pages I have mentioned several things that you can utilise for this purpose. You can charge a 'battery' for good luck to keep in your office. Include a good luck symbol in your logo. Try to open your new business on the day of the new moon, or as near as possible afterwards, but never begin a new venture on a Friday.

Use bay leaves, a symbol of triumph and prosperity, in the following rite to cleanse your office or workplace of any bad or negative aura it may have accrued while bringing in an atmosphere of confidence, creativity and success.

A Ritual to Cleanse the Aura of Your Workplace

Make a small switch by tying a few twigs of the ash tree together with a red thread. Fill a glass bowl with natural water to which a little salt and perfumed oil has been added. You will also need a bowl of bay leaves, a gold candle and some cedar incense sticks. Put a gold cloth on your desk and place everything you have gathered on it.

Walk round the room in an anti-clockwise direction, holding the water in your left hand and the switch in your right. Dip the switch into the water and use it to sprinkle the water around the room as you go, saying, 'Nothing can stand, nothing can stay, by water and earth, all evil away.'

Put the water and switch on your desk. Light the gold candle and cedar incense sticks. Hold the candle in your left hand, and the incense in your right. Walk around the room in a clockwise direction and say, 'By air and by fire, all things I desire shall come, av aki, av aki, av aki.'

Place the candle and incense on your desk. Sprinkle the bay leaves with water using the switch, saying, 'As the bay tree grows, so will I grow; as the bay tree flourishes, so will I prosper; as many as the bay leaves will be my gold coins. Les see kedo, les see kedo, les see kedo.'

Let the candle and incense burn out naturally. Then put the bay leaves under the carpet, by the door, beneath your desk or anywhere else you can secrete them.

The same rite can be performed in the home when you wish to start a family. Just replace the words 'gold coins' with the word 'children'. A receptive, welcoming atmosphere will be created and any obstacles to starting a family will be cleared away.

Children are very important in Gypsy culture. Until recently, when a Romany couple had difficulty in starting a family they would make a pilgrimage to certain places situated on nodes of strong fertilising energy and there spend the night together. The most famous of these is probably the Cerne Abbas Giant in the South-West of England, but there are many more throughout the length and breadth of Britain. Pendle Hill is one; in fact, my granny used to say that there are more of these places in Lancashire than the rest of the country put together. Another powerful but neglected site is on Loxley Chase just outside Sheffield. With a bit of research, you may be able to find a special area where you live.

No matter how great the success, without a loving partner to share it with most people don't feel complete. Perhaps that is why such a large proportion of traditional spellcraft is devoted to attracting and keeping a lover. Although any spell can be adapted to suit either sex, most magic of this kind presupposes that the practitioner is female, probably because most young males find it hard to admit, even to themselves, that they need feminine companionship. It is not until they become mature in their attitude to life that they realise how rewarding a loving relationship is.

A Spell For Attracting Romance

If you wish to attract romance to your life, choose a night when the moon is new or full. Stand next to water – a stream, a well, a river or even a garden pond. Hold a rose or blossom from a fruit tree in your left hand, and a sweet apple cut in half in your right hand. Recite the following:

> Here is a rosebud pink and sweet.
> Here is an apple ready to eat.
> Here is a flower ready to open.
> Here is an apple, true love's token.
> Here is a rose seeking a thorn, here is a love yet to be born.
> Come hands, come teeth, come thorn.

Throw half the apple over your left shoulder without looking. Stick your flower into the ground and eat the other half of the apple.

If you have a fondness for someone and are unsure of their loyalty, the following spell will draw them to you and keep them by your side.

A Spell For Keeping a Loyal Lover

Gather a little earth with your bare hands, and put it into a small bowl that has not been used before. Using a cone-shaped shell, pour a little water taken from a natural source on to the earth. Stir the water into the earth with your finger. Always keeping a picture of your loved one in your mind's eye, say, 'Who can separate this water powerful as the tide, water needs earth to abide. I am you, you are me, we are one.'

Put the bowl to one side for a few days until the earth is dry.
Secretly sprinkle a few grains of the earth on to your loved
one's clothing, into his shoes or where he sits. Put the rest of the
earth into a plant pot and use it to grow your favourite herb.
You can add more earth or compost if you need to in order to
fill up the pot.

Anglers have recently found that female pheromones attract fish.
Long before we ever knew about pheromones, Romany men
would swear that getting a woman to stand quite still, waist deep
in water, would bring the fish around in shoals – not that they
could ever induce a Gypsy woman to do such a thing, you
understand, although I have known one or two Gorga (non-
Romany) ladies who have been talked into it. In this perhaps
overhygienic age it is easy to forget that the function of some
body odour is to attract the opposite sex.

The workings of a woman's body are still considered secret
and to a certain extent sacred in Gypsy society. It is unthinkable
to discuss these things in front of men. Thus magic using the
special power of a woman is of the most deeply occult and
powerful kind, and is never lightly undertaken. One of the most
devastatingly effective spells uses this principle to gain and keep
the person a woman loves. But beware! The effects of this spell
are lifelong and your lover is likely to become totally obsessed
with you.

Female Magic For Attracting a Lifelong Lover

Prepare some food for the person you love, something sweet like cakes, biscuits or pudding. Before cooking add a little of your own body fluids, such as your saliva, sweat or menstrual blood. Stir it into the food mixture with a little whisk made of birch twigs or alternatively a single sturdy birch twig that you have cut yourself. While you are stirring, say:

> I am the nectar, you are the bee.
> I am the honey safe in the tree.
> I have a secret, you have the key.
> Me pander tuti, me pander tuti, me pander tuti com!

Make sure you stir the mixture at least thirty-nine times. When you serve the cake or pudding, put it on a plate with a design of roses around the rim, and hand it to him with your left hand.

Trees are a potent source of energy that can be utilised in various ways. The oak is a great fount of strength; when you are feeling tired or weak, lean against an oak tree for a few moments and feel the strength of the tree seep into your body.

If you are recuperating from an illness, or are just plain tired, the following spell can help to build up your strength and vitality, using the spirit of the oak to invigorate both mind and body.

A Spell For Strength

Take a small loaf of bread, wine, beer or spring water, and a candle – a small one like a tea light will do. The candle can be any colour that makes you happy. Go to an oak tree, and greet it respectfully. Kneel at the base of the oak, break the bread into crumbs and scatter them at the base of the tree, saying, 'I feed you. Please feed me in return.' Empty the liquid, saying, 'Great oak tree, I quench your thirst, quench mine in return.' Light the candle and place it in a safe place near the base of the tree, saying, 'Great oak tree, I pay homage to your wisdom and your strength; bless me with the gift of your spirit.' Lean against the tree. Tell it your troubles. Feel the strength of the oak filling your body, right to the tips of your toes. If possible, sit by the tree until the candle has burned out. (If you can't, stay as long as you can. Blow the candle out and take it with you when you go.) Gently pick a twig, a leaf, an acorn and a square of bark an inch or two long. Wrap them all in a red cloth to take home. Before leaving, be sure to thank the tree sincerely.

Put the things collected from the oak tree into a bowl that has not been used for any other purpose, then cover them with water from a natural source – a river, well or stream. Leave for nine days. Then after nine days take up a little of the water in a shell held in the left hand. Using the first finger of the right hand,

---

There are times when we need to bring a feeling of renewal into our lives; we may be depressed or need fresh impetus to carry on. Exactly the same spell can be used to achieve this, though using the power of the ash tree instead of the oak.

---

anoint each chakra point with water from the shell, making an X sign, saying at each point, 'By the power of this blessing I will grow stronger. *Les see kedo*.' Pour any water that is left in the shell over the top of your head, repeating the same words. Do the same thing every day until the water has all gone.

Healing Herbs and Natural Remedies

Have you ever looked – really looked – into the heart of a flower? The complex patterns and veining, the myriad colours and shades that make up the simplest of blossoms, would be near impossible for any human artist to copy. Even the grass we treat so carelessly has endless variety. Its leaves can be soft and downy, or sharp enough to cut an unwary finger. The flowering seed heads have many subtly beautiful shapes and colours.

When I was a child I loved to lie on the ground and examine the wild flowers, daisies, buttercups and dandelions. Sometimes I felt as if I was as tiny as an insect deep within the centre surrounded by glowing colour. As I grew older, I learned with wonder but no surprise how better technology was showing ever more minute and complex cells and structures pulsating with life, hidden in the most simple-seeming organisms.

The Romanies believe that everything has a spirit and must be treated with respect, even the stones on the ground. Everything can bring good or bad luck, depending on how it is treated or the thoughts that are directed at it. Most of the things on earth are willing to be a friend to man if only man would be a friend to them – none more so than the plants. They provide shelter, fuel and food, oxygenate the air, and of course give us medicine for every condition.

In the past our ancestors relied on the 'doctrine of signatures' to help identify the ailment a plant was good for, relying on the signs placed on the plant itself, such as the spotted lung-like appearance of the lungwort leaf, good for the treatment of coughs. Now science is hard at work trying to find the active chemical elements in plants that bring about the cure. Many of our best-known remedies are plant-based or synthetic versions, such as aspirin, which comes from salacylic acid found in willow bark. Many of these concentrated cures cause side effects, and I fully believe that if all the chemicals found in the plant were used, not just the obvious cure, this would alleviate the side effects dramatically.

Good Places to Collect Healing Herbs

You can pick your herbs carelessly anywhere, or buy them dried from a shop, and you will get good results. But pick them from the right place, at the correct time, and in the right way, and you will capture the essential spirit of the plant, bringing healing to the soul as well as to the body.

Whenever possible the travelling people like to use freshly gathered herbs. It is considered that an illness may be subtly different according to the time of year and phases of the moon, and generally there are several herbal cures for each complaint. The one growing at its peak in the district at the time is the best one to use. Of course herbs are also dried and stored for use when none are available fresh. In this case, extra care is taken to gather them correctly in order to preserve all their virtues.

In this world there are places of good, bad and neutral energies. This should be taken into account when picking your herbs. Most places are neutral and you can happily gather your herbs as long as they look vigorous and healthy.

The bad places should be avoided at all costs. Somewhere beside a busy road, where the verges are polluted by traffic fumes, is obviously bad, as is a location near a field recently sprayed. Not only does the spray drift for a surprisingly long way, poisoning everything it comes into contact with, but it also disturbs the natural energies. The feeling emanating from a sprayed area is one of terrible sadness and despair.

The vicinity of high-tension power lines should also be avoided, although the growth nearby may sometimes look extraordinarily lush. Ancient crossroads were often the scenes of hanging in days gone by; many had a permanent gibbet. Such misery forever scars the energy of a place.

There are some places where a Gypsy will never camp; though they might seem ideal in every way, being lovely and having wood and water in abundance, they are 'moolerie' – the haunts of unpleasant ghosts. These places are not obviously bad in themselves but some instinct tells you not to stop at them. All the above places were resorted to for poisons, abortions and the means to cast curses and unpleasant spells, but never, ever, for medicinal ingredients.

Most areas have at least one special place. It may be near an ancient site, a quiet pool or the banks of a running stream, or it may be a well-used trackway or beside an old twisted tree. It may not be marked in any way, but somehow whenever you go there you feel good, your spirits lift and you feel peaceful. These are the places you should gather your medicinal herbs whenever possible.

Surprisingly, the graveyards around old churches are often good locations. This is especially so if the church is built on a mound or other ancient site. Many such churches have an old yew tree nearby. Although the yew is poisonous, it gives off lovely energies.

You can create your own good place if you have a garden, no matter how small. The most essential thing is to love your garden. Some people love gardening – which is not the same thing. They spray, clip, weed and otherwise torture the place into their own tidy ideal, where nothing is allowed to live unless they put it there.

Your garden should have a life of its own. Let your plants climb and ramble a little, let a little untidiness creep in. There is no need to let the place become a complete jungle, but there should be no disciplined rows of half-hardy annuals, and definitely no weedkiller or slug bait.

Decorate your garden with pots of colourful flowers, strange-shaped lumps of wood or rock, shells, garden ornaments, gnomes if you like, anything pleasing to your eye. Make sure there is water somewhere, even if it is just a shallow bowl for the birds. A fish pond is even better. Your garden should attract wild life of all kinds, and all should be welcome. Plant things that scent the air: old-fashioned roses, honeysuckle, night-scented stock. Plant thyme, rosemary, marjoram and as many other aromatic plants as you can find. Take time to wander about appreciating the scents and sounds. Or just sit. One day you will realise that your garden is humming with life: an oasis of joy in a hard world. Then you will know that you have made your own good place.

Try to pick your herbs in the late morning. The Romanies believe that the essential oils are at their strongest then, before the midday sun starts to evaporate them through the leaves. Roots should be dug very early in the morning, or late evening. By the same token, if you do not need to use the herbs at once, wait until the days just before the full moon for picking the parts above ground, and the dark of the moon for digging roots. Herbs picked up to twenty-four hours after a thunderstorm have extra vibrancy and power.

When picking herbs to dry and store, try to take extra care that the conditions are just right. The plants should be at their peak and completely free from moisture. Roots are best just as the top of the plant is starting to fade and die off. Fasten bunches of herbs tightly with rubber bands, and hang them up in an airy place, away from direct sunlight. Most things take about a week, sometimes a little longer, to dry. Most people like to crush the dried herbs and store them in airtight jars, but if you wish you can leave them hanging in bunches and use them from there.

When you pick the plants, don't pick them right down to the

As I mentioned earlier, you must treat the plants kindly and with respect in order to capture the full spiritual healing essence. When you find a clump of plants you wish to harvest, take a minute or two to tell the group of plants what you are going to do and why. Ask the plants for their aid in healing, tell them how good they are and how they can help you. If you are picking the herbs for a particular person who is unwell at the time, explain this. Mention the person's name and try to picture the person in your mind.

ground. Leave enough stalk and leaves so that the plant can recover, and branch out. Never pick too many plants from one clump. When digging roots replant a good piece to grow next year, and if a plant has already set seed, scatter the seeds about to give them a chance to grow. When you have gathered your herbs, thank the plants sincerely and leave them with a wish that they will soon recover and grow twice as strong.

Preparing Your Potions

INFUSIONS   By far the easiest way of administrating herbs is by making an infusion, or in other words a tea. Use about three teaspoonfuls of dry herbs or a handful of fresh herbs, which you put into a non-metallic jug or pot. Pour over this a pint of boiling water, and leave to stand for a few minutes just as you do when making your usual 'cuppa', then strain and use. This can be taken hot or cold.

DECOCTIONS   For roots, bark and hard seeds, it is better to make a decoction. Use roughly the same amount of herbs to water as for the infusion. Put the herbs in cold water, bring to the boil and simmer for about fifteen minutes. Strain and use. When using dried root or bark it is a good idea to soak them in cold water overnight before making the decoction. All of these can be sweetened with honey or sugar if desired.

SYRUPS   A syrup can be made by melting half a pound of honey with one pint of herbal infusion or decoction. This should be boiled over a low heat until it thickens. The syrup will keep well for a long time. A dessertspoonful should be taken three times a day.

For external use, we can use ointment, oil or a poultice. A poultice is easily made using the hot macerated herb, on a bandage or clean cloth, applied to the affected spot. Sometimes the herb can be mixed with a little hot mashed potato, or thick oat porridge, especially when a large poultice is needed.

OILS   Oils too are very simple to make. Fill a jar tightly with fresh herbs. Cover the herbs well with any good pure vegetable oil – olive oil is ideal – and seal the jar. This should then be left to stand in a warm spot; a sunny windowsill is ideal. Shake the jar daily. After about three weeks the goodness of the herb will have seeped into the oil. Strain well and bottle.

My favourite oil is St John's wort. After a few weeks it magically turns from light brown to a lovely red. It is one of the most useful oils, being good for most things from burns and bruises to grazes and rashes.

Most herbs are not as powerful as modern drugs, of course, and usually there is plenty of leeway between a safe dose and one that is too strong. As a general rule a small wine glass of infusion or decoction three times a day is correct. However, although my experience of the treatments in this book has been favourable, please remember that none of the remedies are intended to replace professional medical advice. If you have any allergies or if you are pregnant, I would suggest that you talk to a doctor before trying any of these remedies.

OINTMENTS   Ointments can be made using a base of good pure fat such as lard or white Vaseline. Melt this over a gentle heat, add as much crushed herbs as the fat can take (usually about one ounce of herb to eight ounces of base), then simmer gently for about fifteen minutes. Strain and pour into jars to set. If you want a harder ointment, remelt and add a little beeswax.

Once goose fat was much prized as a base for ointments of all kinds, though the Romany people swear that the best base of all is hedgehog fat. It is said that the fat of the hedgehog never sets, and its powers of penetration are second to none. There is also a small-greenish coloured gland found when gutting the hedgehog, and it contains the precious hedgehog oil. This oil is held in the highest regard, having almost mythical powers of healing and being used as a cure for almost everything from eye ailments to rheumatics.

Some Useful Remedies

Everyone using herbs will have their favourite remedies, the ones most useful for their own lifestyle. The following are some of my own favourites.

COUGHS AND COLDS   The Romany are a pretty robust lot, well used to adversity and harsh conditions of all kinds, but theirs is a hard and strenuous life. Most of the work done requires a great deal of manual labour. At home there is water to carry, wood to gather, and it is no joke cooking over a smoky fire. Sometimes in wet weather it is impossible to get dry for days on end.

All this leads to coughs, colds and rheumatism. There are many remedies for these complaints. My four basics for coughs are coltsfoot, lungwort, hyssop and mallow. If I had to choose one I would prefer lungwort, especially for chesty coughs. An infusion can be made from any one of these, or a mixture of several or all of them in equal parts. For a dry cough add a little skullcap.

Another favourite is honey and onion mixture, which is good when the cough is accompanied by a sore throat or cold. It may seem a strange combination, but it is effective and palatable. Melt half a jar of honey over a gentle heat. Roughly chop a medium-sized onion and add it to the honey. Bring it to the boiling point and simmer for about five minutes until the onion is soft. There is no need to strain the mixture. Take a teaspoonful as often as needed.

A teaspoonful of cayenne pepper well mixed into half a cup of black treacle stops coughs quickly. Try a little first to gauge the strength of

---

The hedgehog is very much admired by the Gypsy people. He is considered clever and brave, loyal to his family and versatile in gaining a living just like the Gypsy himself. The meat of the hedgehog is health-giving and credited with keeping the mind and spirit young in old age. It was mostly eaten in the autumn, when the young were grown and the animals good and fat, ready for winter hibernation. Nowadays the poor little hedgehog is becoming rarer, a victim of slug bait and road accidents, and is not eaten so often.

---

the mixture. It should be quite fiery but not too overpowering. Take a teaspoonful as needed. Cayenne is an ingredient of many commercial cough mixtures.

For colds an infusion of yarrow is one of the best remedies. A clove of garlic peeled and sniffed often helps to get rid of cold germs. It is best to hang it around the neck on a strong thread, but this often gets rid of your friends as well as the cold. Raw garlic rubbed over a cold sore will help to get rid of it quickly.

RHEUMATISM Rheumatism can never be really cured, but it can be made more bearable and considerably eased. An infusion of nettle, bean pods, dandelion or couch grass can help. Willow bark is very good for easing the pain, bringing down the temperature and easing inflammation. Cut a willow stick about the length of the patient's arm from the elbow to the tip of the middle finger and about as thick as their finger. The bark should be stripped from the stick and make into a decoction with one pint of water.

Cider vinegar can work miracles in some cases. A tablespoonful in a small amount of hot water should be taken each morning before breakfast. This can be sweetened with honey if liked. I have known all symptoms of rheumatism to disappear after a few months of taking cider vinegar, and it is especially good in warding off the disease if taken when the first symptoms appear.

CUTS, BRUISES, SPRAINS, BURNS AND BOILS Cuts, bruises and burns are an everyday hazard of travelling life. Burns should be held under plain cold water as soon as the burn happens, but St John's wort oil or lavender oil will soothe the sting and promote rapid healing.

Wounds should be washed in a solution of one tablespoon of salt, preferably sea salt, to one pint of water. For clean wounds nothing heals better than woundwort, which is best used as freshly crushed leaves on a sticking plaster or bandage. Woundwort will cure even hard-to-heal cuts and sores quickly. I knew one man who had a deep cut on his knuckle for several weeks. It wouldn't heal because every time he moved his finger the cut reopened. It was treated with woundwort, and after three days the knuckle was almost completely healed.

Because of the remarkably quick way this herb closes wounds it should not be used on dirty or infected sores. These should first be cleansed and treated with a drawing herb such as plantain. Fresh woundwort leaves soon get rid of gumboils and mouth ulcers, when chewed lightly and held on the sore spot.

Plantain is very good at taking the painful swelling out of a whitlow or boil. Crush the fresh leaves, and bandage on to the inflammation.

Comfrey is a wonderful remedy for sprains and even broken bones. The root should be simmered until it turns into a sticky pulp. Leave this to cool and use as a poultice on the hurt part. A tea made from the leaves can help internal injuries.

Bruises can be helped by dabbing with a strong cool infusion of marigold or St John's wort, or the oil of either of these herbs. The fresh crushed leaf of a houseleek dabbed on a bruise will also help healing.

NERVES AND HEADACHES Most Gorgio (non-Romanies) think the Gypsy has a carefree life and would be surprised to know the amount of nervous tension he is under every day. Apart from having to be self-reliant in earning a living, there is the constant racial harassment, both subtle and overt, as well as the ever present knowledge that one can be moved on at any time of the day or night. Because of this, many travellers develop a habit of bolting their food down as quickly as possible before the meal can be interrupted, which of course leads to stomach troubles.

When the nerves are frayed the following herbal tea can be used instead of the supermarket variety. It soothes the nerves and can help the general well-being. Take equal parts of sage, marjoram, rosemary and thyme. Mix well together and use about three teaspoonfuls to a pot. Make the tea in the usual way.

For really bad nervous ailments use the above herbs as a base then add equal parts of skullcap, vervain and St John's wort herbs and valerian root. The valerian root should be soaked overnight in a cup full of cold water. Then put all your herbs together with the valerian root and the water in which it was soaked into a pan. Cover with the correct amount of water for an infusion. Bring to the boil and simmer gently for one minute. Strain when cool and take a wineglass of it three times a day for a week, then twice a day morning and night.

As the condition improves weaken the mixture by leaving out first the valerian, then later the skullcap. A word about valerian root: it is an excellent nervine, but it can be just as strong as Valium, so it should be used with care. The above mixture is the best I know for nervous ailments. It has also been used with great success to treat the terrible symptoms of alcoholism, and help to overcome the craving for drink.

Of course nervous tension brings many headaches. I have already mentioned willow bark, which is also excellent for headaches and will cure the most severe cases. For migraine nothing can beat feverfew. A few leaves should be eaten between slices of bread. This is because the leaves can irritate the mouth if used alone.

To help sleeplessness a hot tea of either skullcap or camomile will help. The two should not be used together though, as this can cause constipation. In severe cases of insomnia, especially when accompanied by pain, a teaspoonful of poppy syrup can help. The syrup is made as described on page 169 using the seed heads of the wild red poppy. Some people say all parts of the poppy can be used.

INDIGESTION Indigestion should first be treated with a strong mint tea drunk hot by the cupful. This can be sweetened with honey or sugar. Angelica too makes a good tea for this purpose, and is very warming. The stalk, leaves or seeds can be used.

Cramps in the stomach or the limbs can be treated with cramp bark.

CIRCULATION   For all circulatory problems, and even for a weak heart, hawthorn berries are a good safe remedy that can be taken for long periods of time.

CONSTIPATION   For curing constipation safe remedies include rhubarb, all plums, but especially sloes, and liquorice. Sloe jam can be made as a palatable cure, but should only be used for this purpose. Apples can sometimes act against diarrhoea, as can meadow sweet, loostrife or hops. For piles and haemorrhoids pilewort ointment is very good.

EYES   Sore eyes are often the result of being round a smoky fire. A
well-strained infusion of eyebright makes a soothing eyewash.
Marigold flowers are sometimes used for this purpose too.

FOOT PROBLEMS   In the days of horse-drawn wagons the Romany
walked and ran beside the horse for many miles. As many of them
wore second-hand, often ill-fitting shoes, they suffered with their feet,
especially in later years. In fact this is still a complaint among the
Romanies, mostly among the women, who still walk many miles
hawking.

When the feet are tired and sore the soft, cool leaves of the butter
burr can be put in the shoes to help ease the pain. Chilblains can be
healed with well-crushed snowdrop bulbs. For corns, try soaking ivy
leaves in vinegar overnight and then apply them to the corn.

TOOTHACHE   There is nothing worse than a toothache when there
is no hope of getting to a dentist. Clove oil applied neat to the bad
tooth will help to ease the pain. Friar's balsam sometimes serves the
same purpose. A poultice of salt wrapped in a cloth and heated in the
oven then held to the cheek will also ease the pain. An old-fashioned
cure is as follows. Take a sheet of strong brown paper. Form the paper
into a cone and twist the narrow end. Stand the cone on its base on a
cold plate. Light the tapered end of the cone. When the paper has
completely burned away remove the ashes. There should be a small
amount of a brown, tarry substance left on the plate. This should be
applied to the affected tooth.

TINNITUS   One of the results of our noisy world is the increase in tinnitus, or ringing in the ears. This is often caused by noise damage to the nerves of the inner ear, and it can cause a great deal of stress to the sufferer. Unfortunately there doesn't seem to be any known cure, but sometimes it can be helped.

Black cohosh and goldenseal are two herbs that are most used, either alone or mixed together. Some others that have sometimes helped are ground ivy (otherwise known as ale hoof), periwinkle and blue flag root. The cohosh and goldenseal both come as fine powders. Only the tip of a teaspoonful should be used three times a day. This can be mixed in water but is very unpleasant. Alternatively it can be made into a pill with a little soft bread, and swallowed whole, or it can be used to fill gelatine capsules. The other three herbs are made into an infusion as usual.

WOMEN'S HEALTH   To the Romany, children are the greatest blessing on earth and large families are still desirable. There are many laws and traditions surrounding pregnancy and childbirth, and of course remedies for the various ailments that accompany that condition.

The most popular and effective aid to an easy labour is raspberry leaf tea. This is even made into tablets as a commercial product. This tea should be drunk through the last month of pregnancy, with the juice of an orange squeezed into the cup.

For morning sickness there are several teas that can be tried, including peppermint, hops, meadowsweet, black horehound and camomile. These can be used singly or as a mixture of several of these herbs in equal parts.

Miscarriage is a tragedy that can be brought about by many different causes. Unfortunately there is very little that natural medicine can do to prevent it happening. Unlike abortives, of which there seem to be many in the plant world, I have come across few plant remedies that claim to stop a miscarriage. Rest and good food are the best preventives, with an antispasmodic such as cramp bark being taken three times a day, as well as a nervine like skullcap or valerian to relax the patient.

Sometimes there is difficulty in breast-feeding, especially with a first child. The seeds of caraway and fennel can be used to help the milk to flow. It is a pleasant and safe aid, which should be made as a decoction and drunk by the mother three times a day.

For period pains, sometimes a general painkiller such as the willow bark tea can help, or even a warming drink of mint or angelica. Cramp bark is also effective in calming the terrible spasms that often occur at this time.

WARTS   I am always being asked, 'Can you cure warts?' Warts are strange things. They can easily be 'charmed' away, and some people used to specialise in wart charming and were often quite famous because of it. My husband's aunt, Bethany Price, was one of these. People would go to her from far and wide to be cured of their warts. It was said she would take their penny, say one or two strange words, and by the time they reached home the warts had disappeared. Old Bethany was never short of one or two tasty delicacies on the dinner table, donated by grateful clients.

There are two simple wart charms you can try. The person with the wart must find someone to 'buy' the wart from him. The buyer should give the sufferer a small coin, saying, 'I buy this wart to throw away, to trouble no one from this day.' The person with the wart should then bury the coin secretly, having first sprinkled it with salt. The wart should disappear within a week.

The second charm should be done in secret when the moon is waning. A small piece of raw meat should be rubbed over the wart whilst saying, 'Meat to wart, wart to meat,' three times. The meat should then be buried in the ground whilst saying, 'It is not meat I bury here, but that which troubles me severe.' The wart will be gone in a few days.

There are some effective plant cures for warts. Three of the best are greater celandine, dandelion and spurge. The milky juice from the stems of any of these plants can be rubbed on the wart daily. It may take several weeks to work, but your patience will be rewarded as the wart first turns black, then shrinks and eventually falls off.

STEAM TREATMENT One remedy largely forgotten now is steam treatment. Travelling in Ireland I was intrigued by the little stone beehive-shaped buildings. On enquiring, I was told they were sweathouses. Many cultures have their own versions of the sweathouse, including the American Indian sweat lodge and the Scandinavian sauna. Generally, stones are heated on a fire and then carried into a small tent or room, which is well sealed. Cold water is thrown on to the hot stones, and sometimes herbs are added too. The resulting steam is very hot. It wasn't usual to stay for more than an hour in the steam, as the first effect can be a great feeling of weakness on emerging. The participant was then wrapped warmly and advised to rest for a while.

The steam bath is a wonderful treatment to ease aches and pains. A simple way of getting a similar effect is to sit on a wooden chair with a bowl of boiling water underneath. Wrap yourself, chair and all in a large blanket so that the steam can't escape. Appropriate herbs can be added to the water, for instance, nettle, hyssop or marjoram for rheumatism, rue and comfrey for sprains, rosemary to deep-clean the skin, lavender for headaches. Feverfew is particularly effective for cystitis when used in this way. This treatment can be used for many complaints, depression, nerves, asthma and other chest complaints and many others; just use the herbs appropriate to the condition. A little aromatherapy oil can be added to the water if you wish.

The above treatment was popular at the turn of the century, when a hot brick was placed in a metal bowl and sprinkled with water to make the steam. It is important to wrap up warmly after the treatment and try to put your feet up for an hour as well.

A Few Little Romany Beauty Tips

The sight of a wrinkled, weather-beaten Gypsy woman is not the best advert for face cream, but there are some notable exceptions. I had a wonderful honorary aunt by the name of Marrilla May. In her youth she had been a great beauty; it was said that a famous artist had wanted to paint her as the Gypsy Rose, but fears for her virtue put a stop to that.

This lady was well into her eighties when I knew her, but in spite of her hard, toil-filled life she could pass for someone thirty years younger. I was always a favourite of hers because I never tired of listening to her tales and stories. One day when I was complaining that my skin was becoming roughened by the weather she gave me her recipe for skin cream, swearing that it was the secret of her lovely smooth complexion.

Marrilla used her cream as a hand and body cream, as well as a cleanser and moisturiser. She never used soap on her face. In the morning she would splash her face with water then pat it dry with her fingertips. She swore that to bathe the face in the early morning dew was the best beauty treatment one could wish for.

At night she would cleanse her skin using her cream, then rub her face with a rough, damp flannel. Then she would freshen it with a mixture of half witch hazel and half rose water before nourishing it with her cream. If her skin seemed dull or rough she would scrub her face with ordinary sugar granules on damp skin. She always recommended the sugar treatment to anyone suffering from acne too.

Marrilla May's Face Cream

2 tablespoons beeswax

4 tablespoons white petroleum jelly

2 tablespoons lanolin

6 tablespoons wheatgerm oil

6 tablespoons almond oil

1 teaspoon tincture benzoin

1 teaspoon tincture myrrh

½ teaspoon borax

crushed houseleek

elderflowers or rose petals, according to season

Melt the petroleum jelly, lanolin and beeswax over a gentle heat. Add as many elderflowers or rose petals as the liquid will hold. Simmer very gently for twenty minutes.

Add the crushed houseleek and simmer for a further ten minutes. Strain and return to the heat then add the wheatgerm and almond oil. Dissolve the borax in a very little warm water and add to the mixture, beating well. Remove from the heat and continue beating until the mixture cools slightly. Add the benzoin and myrrh, beat until the cream sets – you can use a food processor for the last bit. Apply in the evening (but, as with any beauty treatment, do not persist if you develop any allergic reactions).

HAIR TREATMENTS   One thing the Romany women are justly proud of is their lustrous hair. Coconut oil has always been very popular to nourish the roots and make the hair shine, and a rinse made from a strong sage tea is often used to keep the hair dark well into old age. When shampooing the hair it is often difficult to spare enough water to rinse all the suds away really thoroughly when every precious drop has to be carried, but a tablespoon of malt vinegar in the last

Another of Marrilla May's treatments was a nourishing facemask made with an egg yolk and a teaspoonful of almond oil well mixed together. This was left on the face for at least twenty minutes, longer if possible. This mask can be used two or three times a week.

rinsing water leaves hair dark and shining; a tablespoon of lemon juice does the same for blond hair.

Incidentally, it is not true that all Romanies are dark and swarthy. Some of the families we know as of 'the true black blood' are blond and fair-skinned, or red-haired.

HAND TREATMENTS Living a Romany life, it is hard to keep one's hands at all nice. Working on the land, hauling scrap, and of course cooking over an open fire all tend to leave the hands ingrained with dirt.

Rough or really dirty hands can benefit from the following treatment. Warm a little olive oil (making sure that it is not hot enough to burn) and smooth it over your hands, then pour a little sugar into your palms and scrub this all over your hands. Rinse with warm water.

You will be surprised how this will lift the dirt out and leave the skin feeling soft. A little oatmeal on wet hands also works quite well.

To keep age spots at bay massage your hands with castor oil morning and night. Help to keep nails healthy with a little almond oil massaged into the cuticles after a bath.

TEETH Teeth can be kept gleaming white by brushing them with ordinary salt or bicarbonate of soda on a damp toothbrush. In the old days wood ash from the fire was used in the same way. Lavender infusion makes a good mouthwash that helps to keep the gums healthy.

Conclusion

Natural items such as flowers, shells and stones are very important in Gypsy magic. There are some that, if examined, are marked with meaningful symbols, and these are considered to be much more powerful than any man-made paraphernalia, being the direct gift of the earth. There is an unimagined power all around us: the currents of zee earth energy, the beautiful complex natural things that make up our world.

The so-called 'rational' man of today often thinks that he has no need of what he calls superstitious nonsense, and may laugh at shamans, medicine men and Gypsies. But who will be proved right, I wonder: modern man whose every step along the road of progress seems to bring the Earth closer to death, or people like the shamans and the Gypsies, who cherish nature and work with her in every possible way?

Further Reading

DIVINATION BOOKS

Easons, Cassandra, *The Complete Book of Tarot* (Piatkus, 1999)

Gardini, Maria, *Palmistry* (Ebury Press, 1988)

Moor, Michael P, *A Manual of Modern Palmistry* (Aurum Press, 1996)

Pennick, Nigel, *The Complete Illustrated Guide to the Runes* (Element Books, 1999)

Regardie, Israel, *How to Make and Use Talismans* (The Aquarian Press, 1972)

Sepharial, *The Book of Charms and Talismans* (W. Foulsham & Co, undated)

Sharman-Burk, Juliet, *Understanding the Tarot* (Rider, 1998)

Taylor, Ken, *Tarot for Today* (London House, 2000)

Wild, Julian, *Grimoire of Chaos Magic* (The Sorcerer's Apprentice Press, undated)

HERBS AND HEALING

When picking herbs in the wild, it is important to identify the plants correctly, so a good flower book is essential:

Chief, Roberto, *The Macdonald Encyclopaedia of Medicinal Plants* (Macdonald, 1984)

Keble Martin, W, *The Concise British Flora in Colour* (Ebury Press, 1965)

If you wish to grow your own herbs from seed, you can contact:

John Chambers Wild Flower Seeds
15 Westleigh Road
Barton Seagrave
Kettering
Northants NN15 5AJ
UK
(Tel: 01933 652562)

Dried medicinal herbs and tinctures etc can be bought by mail order from

Godfrey Brothers
29 Worm Gate
Boston
Lincolnshire PE21 6NR
UK
(Tel: 01205 367457)